THE EMPATHY CHRONICLES

Rejoice With Those Who rejoice, Weep
With Those Who Weep, and Suffer
With Those Who Suffer

Terry Jamieson

THE EMPATHY CHRONICLES

Rejoice With Those Who rejoice, Weep With Those Who Weep, and Suffer With Those Who Suffer

Terry Jamieson

Christian Publishing House
Cambridge, Ohio

Christian Publishing House
Professional Conservative Christian Publishing of the Good News!

Unless otherwise stated, Scripture quotations are from *The Holy Bible, Updated American Standard Version (UASV)®*, Copyright © 2016 by Christian Publishing House, Professional Conservative Christian Publishing of the Good News!

THE EMPATHY CHRONICLES: Rejoice With Those Who rejoice, Weep With Those Who Weep, and Suffer With Those Who Suffer

ISBN-10: 1-945757-35-3

ISBN-13: 978-1-945757-35-8

Photo Credits:

Cover: Morgan Weistling (http://www.morganweistling.com/)

We cannot avoid the world. As Christians, we must go out
and demonstrate the love of God in our actions.

Table of Contents

The Empathy Chronicles

Introduction

This is a book of thoughts. Perhaps these are thoughts compiled over a lifetime. I decided that I would not limit myself to meetings and seminars as a platform to communicate with those people I worked with daily in my role as a school administrator. Instead, I arrived at my desk each morning and sent out a daily thought in hopes that each and every person in our building would know what I was thinking. Leadership is only effective if it is followed loyally. People believe in who they trust. Communication fosters trust. All other leaders are followed out of fear or as a survival mechanism.

This is also a book of hope. It is only through our relationships that we find hope. We begin by finding it in God and then each other. At the core of every successful team is the sense of openness, knowing one another, sharing in the journey that is life. This is a book for leaders, teachers, parents, anyone that is granted the great responsibility of decision-making and mentorship.

This was my daily journal for an entire school year, and Included within these pages are a personal testimony. I hope that you will see my love for God, my daily search for the meaning of life, and ultimately my message to the community of educators and corporate leaders that are working in a society that has excused God from the institutions that should make us strong.

There were 176 days in that school year. The book is not divided up by school quarters or by months. Instead, it is offered to you simply and candidly, just as it was daily.

Christian Publishing House: Within this publication, there will be footnotes that may add additional thoughts that expound on what is being said or qualifies what is being said. These notes will begin with **CPH**: ...

Day 1

I could not sleep last night. Of course, today is the first day of school, and I am reminded of my childhood. As a child, I was frightened of the thought that I would be leaving home to board a bus and ride for over an hour through our rural landscape with strangers. The idea of school had no relevance at that time. It was only an intimidating requirement of life, and although my own home was dysfunctional, I had no idea how dysfunctional school could be. It was a microcosm of society, filled with the imperfections and emotional pitfalls of life. I think as I sat on the bus staring out the window and holding a tiny bag of school supplies, I may have been praying for protection and for someone to care for me since my mother could not come along.

And so this morning in my role as a principal, I am reminded that our bus fleet left at dawn to tour this large district and pick up the human lives that are gifted to each of us who chose education as a profession. So many are afraid right now, probably staring out windows wondering what will happen today, who they will meet, who will help them survive, and who will extend the universal need of love.

I found myself in tears as I wrote these words. I too am afraid somewhat. Will I make the right decisions? Will my empathy be obvious to children and teachers? Can I be brimming over with compassion yet be strong enough to teach them character and instill discipline?

God, where are You this morning? Are You embracing this building in spite of the fact that we as a culture have invited You to stay away? I love You and cannot do this without Your great guidance. Forgive me now for my own imperfections, and fill me with perfect love and vision. May we end this day better than it began.

I sent an email to the teachers this morning.

Good morning:

I am thankful that God has allowed me to be in this role. I could not sleep last night because, of course, today was the first day.

I found myself praying that we could all enter the building with the hope that we truly understand how important we are to these children. I am fortunate to be in the company of all of you, and I need you to be patient with me as I learn how to help each of you and serve you. Please know that I have the best intentions and will pour my heart into this.

I am also lucky to have my assistant principal. She is an outstanding school leader. She shares in the visions so imperative to helping people. This morning expect glitches and spilled milk, but let's just roll with the issues and improve together. There will be class changes as we attempt to consolidate some schedule issues.

Take roll and talk school with your students until 9:00 a.m., and then I will spend time with them in the gym. You should dismiss at around 8:55 a.m. to the gym.

May God bless us all.

Day 2

Yesterday at the first assembly, I demanded the students embrace the concept of character. I asked them to understand that success is spiritual, and athletic ability and beauty were merely relative, but character was imperative. I asked them to be Good Samaritans and if they were offended by that word to call their lawyers. I felt I was arrogant. My intention is to bring God back into this school and force people to understand that our very survival is dependent upon knowing God.

Early this morning, I watched a boy push another boy in a wheelchair through the halls and to a classroom. I asked their names and learned they were brothers. I became emotional looking in their eyes, realizing they would rather be anywhere but here. I hope the other students and teachers can look upon these two boys as blessed by God because they are meek, and they will inherit the earth.

I have a teacher in my building who works with severely handicapped students, and quite frankly, she is a saint. In fact, her two helpers are also saints. These children range in severity of need from minor to major. One of the students cannot talk. Communication is relegated to grunts and hand gestures, yet these three women are remarkable in the ways they hand out love and attention while trying to teach even the most rudimentary human skills. The world outside of their classroom has no idea what these women do for a living or how hard their jobs are. I am emotional standing outside their door; realizing prayer is what they need. I almost asked one of them if she was a Christian, but I hesitated. It is a shame that question cannot be asked. Perhaps I will find out as I get to know them.

This morning a child walked by me who has not bathed in several days, or at least that is what I ascertain judging from body odor and soiled clothing. He had a look on his face that belied an enormous void in his soul. I know his name and called him to me to say hello and ask how he was. He could not look into my eyes and spoke so softly that I wondered if he was afraid to communicate or somehow afraid of people. It could be that his opinion of himself was so pitiful that he simply could not relate to someone else. At the very moment he walked away, I wondered if prayer would be enough. Is this faithless of me? How can my words and requests put clean clothes on his body or wash his skin? I felt helpless as he walked away. It was a sick feeling.

I played Simon Says with the sixth grade today and won. A little girl demanded a rematch with a smile on her face. Two boys who have been silent and somewhat sullen since we started yesterday said goodbye to me and called me sir. I feel I will sleep well tonight. May our God bless us with the strength and courage to invite Him back into this building.

I am in prayer right now, taking inventory of my words and actions today, hoping I was a good role model, a Christian in every sense.

Day 3

I have the thought this morning that teachers cannot be trained in college. No degree can truly lend the training necessary to become a teacher. Those people who possess what I call the Rainbow Personality can do the job and do it well. In fact, without a diverse set of intellectual skills, it is impossible to teach. How to define those skills becomes somewhat difficult, but I do know empathy and strength of character are at the top of the list, along with assertiveness and fluid articulation. So many people get into this profession, thinking teaching is holding knowledge and being able to share it, but of course, they do not last long. Some should not be teachers. They seem to grow apathetic or bitter, and their weakened souls soon erode the lives of others.

This morning as I reflect on the past two days, I find myself thinking about the many gestures of kindness and patience dis- played by the teachers in this building. So many of them truly possess the Rainbow Personality.

After lunch, I walked the boy in the wheelchair back to class. He sang, "You are my sunshine." I commented to his teacher that there is nothing in the world to be down about after you walk this child.

I was just briefed regarding a group of seriously at-risk students. Their files are here before me, and after reading a few lines, it is rather depressing to digest the dark worlds of these children, where they live, the baggage they bring to school, and problems that have been placed on their shoulders by their parents. I note here that one particular boy is being raised by parents who cannot read as well as he can, and they both suffer from substance abuse problems that have simply destroyed their home and any possibility of hope. I cannot begin to conjure a prayer that seems to meet their needs, so all I can do is turn them over to God and hope His will is done in their lives. This brings me the thought that perhaps caring is sometimes all a person can do. That is enough in those helpless times when we search for ways to repair damaged lives.

May God bless us again this day to have eyes that see.

Day 4

So many administrators speak of curriculum. For much of my career, it has been a dynamic word, and it seems that many in the profession think teachers should be zoned in on it, forsaking all else. In fact, I worked with an administrator who was convinced I was unprepared to be a building leader because I had not attended enough professional development seminars dealing with curriculum. He failed to recommend me for a job I was coveting because as he said, "You are not well-versed in the area of curriculum." I asserted that curriculum is vital but ever changing, and eventually students will have so much information readily available through technology that teachers will no longer be the holders of knowledge. I submitted to him that teachers should be more in tune with people-management issues, classroom management issues, and ultimately the psychology of learning.

I am convinced teaching is a spiritual calling. People must realize that helping a child learn depends on the relationship more than curriculum. I define curriculum as what is being taught — mathematics, science, communication arts, and the deeper intricacies that lie within — but to teach, a person must first know the student and make a connection. That is an area that is hard for someone who is data-driven or focusing on curriculum as opposed to the individual.

Here is where godly people must enter the profession. To become a Christian is to have a relationship with God and to ground that bond in faith. Making one's life a living sacrifice is to embrace the concept of living for others. A teacher who lives for students — who lives for their success both educationally and more importantly spiritually — is a teacher who truly can shape a person for the future.

Curriculum is essential but empathy is imperative, and those who possess the gift of empathy are truly the best teachers.

May God help us all to love unconditionally, lead by example, give our lives away as living sacrifices, and offer each child in this building the chance to overcome life's obstacles through relationship.

May God bless us again today.

Day 5

Just one word or gesture is all it takes. Even after 40 years, I can still hear the words of teachers echoing in my mind. I wonder if educators really grasp that words and gestures are enduring, especially when spoken within the educational process. I believe God intends for teachers to be vessels of edification. Of course, there are times that honesty requires painful words, but even then, the words of instruction can be laced with encouragement. The end result could be a life transformed or even saved. I commented a few days ago to our teachers in a meeting that we should enter the school year with several rules to live by as we wrap our brains around the monumentally important job of molding human beings.

(1) Never chastise a student in front of peers. If you must be in a position to discipline, then bear in mind it can be done without dragging a spirit out and exposing it to others and then trampling upon it.

(2) Be honest and fair, and then be complimentary.

(3) Get to know students, and then search for ways to build up self-esteem.

(4) Grasp firmly the concept of protecting another person's soul. If you grapple for this, then you do not get it.

(5) Look upon each student as a future adult, and ask yourself if you would speak to the student 30 years from now the way you just spoke to him or her in school.

It is hard to say what causes the issues of adulthood, though an educated person can be fairly certain that social environment plays a role in the outcomes of lives. Choices are made because we have free will, but in the grand scheme, I believe people can be scarred for life by the words of a harsh or bitter teacher, and people can be lifted higher than clouds by the kindness of a Christian teacher.

I pray this day that God will strengthen me with the clear mindset of an empathetic teacher and that my words will lift people to another level of contentment.

Day 6

Christ actually gave the profession of teaching a stern warning if you look closely at His words in the Book of Mathew. He said, "Whoever stumbles one of these little ones who have faith in me, it would be better for him to have hung around his neck a millstone that is turned by a donkey and to be drowned in the depth of the sea."[1] (Matthew 18:6; UASV)

I do not know how a person can read those words and not feel the full force of compassion spilling from the heart of Jesus Christ. I am certain any teacher who chooses to create a learning environment that is embedded in the fierce desire to help children become spiritually strong will never be accused of causing one to fall.

Although the usage of the word millstone seems harsh to some, I am confident Christ was trying to drive home the point that being a role model is essential, and both our words and actions can lead to the success or demise of children. Therefore, He wanted us to take this profession seriously. Was He speaking of teachers when He said this? Actually, He was speaking to teachers, parents, or anyone else who has direct influence over children, which, of course, is the entire population, but at the end of the day, it is safe to say that teachers are in a role that should be held to a higher standard.

This morning an elementary child of no more than seven or eight years old walked past me and smiled. She said hello, and although weighted down by a huge backpack and obviously already tired from a long bus ride, she nonetheless looked at me with the eyes of someone who could know no other way but kindness. I am obligated by Christ to return that same smile and kindness with an even greater measure poured over her delicate soul. At that moment, the verse in Matthew came to mind, not because I am intimidated by the concept of having a millstone around my neck if I cause a child to sin, but because I realize the great

---

[1] **CPH:** The *little ones* spoken of here are those who believe in Jesus Christ. The passage is actually referring to the penalty for any Christian who may cause other believers to "sin," namely, violate their own Christian consciences, i.e., cause them to stumble spiritually. Generally, this would happen with a Christian who is seen as being spiritually mature and looked up to in that way, who would stumble a believer, even unintentionally, who is less mature spiritually. Therefore, one could draw an implication that even outside of the church, if any adult, especially those in leadership roles (teachers, counselors, parents, etc.), who would cause a younger one to sin or violate their conscience, they too would be judged for such things.

honor before me of protecting them, and that is what gives me hope this day.

Thank God, that Christ was the best teacher of all.

Day 7

The teaching methods of Christ were amazing. He had the perfect approach to opening the eyes of people to obvious issues and simple solutions. He offered analogies and storytelling that related real-world issues to literally anyone from any culture. There is no possibility that an individual living in this modern and technologically advanced day and age could look at the teachings of Christ and say they would not apply to their lives. In other words, His teachings were relevant. Even now, the words He so eloquently spoke long ago to a culture that was truly ignorant of His love are relevant.

I am confident that student or teacher apathy is often caused by the feelings that curriculum is not relevant. If a student cannot see the practical importance of subject matter, then apathy is sure to follow. If a teacher cannot enjoy coming to the classroom daily, then surely apathy is the end result. It is when we see the relevance of learning that we bloom. Christ made the lessons of life relevant, and He enamored His Apostles. Even those people who did not follow Him either respected Him for His knowledge or feared Him because He could bring about change.

I walked by a classroom this morning and heard a teacher telling a personal story. Her students were glued to every word. The room was quiet except for her voice. The story was relevant not only to her objective but also to the lives of every child in that room.

We should come to school every day with the intent of giving relevance to life. Living for God is the only way for this to occur. I have learned that devout believers radiate life relevance daily.

How can we teach if we are not living for God?

Day 8

I teach education courses at the local community college, and I began a lecture by asking each person to conduct a self-inventory and ask themselves this question: What do people see when they look at me? I told my son long ago that he should not go through life with the attitude of not caring what people thought of him because eventually, people will stop thinking of you. So it is that I think educators should be cognizant of the image they portray to the public, especially parents.

Bear in mind that so many people are lost. They have broken lives caused by poor choices and by circumstances beyond their control. They might suffer from low self-esteem, lack of education, substance abuse issues, domestic violence, poverty, and the list goes on and on. When all is said and done, they all too often live their lives vicariously through their children. People who are disgusted with their lives look upon their children as the last chance to find value in life. They want their children to be the best athletes or students or even find popularity and acceptance. Our empathy must be extended to parents. It is sobering to sit in the presence of parents who are unemployed, suffering from a wretched vice, uneducated, or perhaps depressed, and listen as they cry out from the soul to be heard or understood. Realize that the vast majority of people love their children and want a better life for their children than they had. It should be the goal of all parents.

Therefore, it is today that I pray for the ability to understand and empathize with all people, even those who might be angry with me or not comprehend the decisions I make regarding their children. I cannot go through my career trying to save every child, who has no regard for their parent. My vision should be to reach out to anyone and everyone connected to this school. My desire to teach should extend to all people and not just those under this roof each day. We should care what parents think of us. They are included in this equation.

Day 9

Post-secondary education cannot prepare a person to be a teacher. In fact, the education programs at universities and colleges are simply inadequate. I realize my assertion seems negative, but through years of experience in education, I am convinced that teacher candidates would be better served by having internships that last more than one semester and place the candidate in an actual teaching role, monitored, of course, by a fulltime professional educator. The profession of teaching has more to do with psychology than data.

When I completed degree requirements in the field of educational leadership and policy analysis to become a building leader, I was struck by how detached the world of higher education seemed to be from the realities of public schools. The data and research used by higher education is profound and contains merit, and I definitely see the need to pay close attention to differentiated instruction and best methods. What I think is lost in the grand scheme is the true understanding that teachers must possess skills of assertiveness and articulation as well as understanding the intricate psychology of the human mind. Higher education requires little training in speech and creativity, which, of course, are two imperative talents in teaching. After all, if you are a boring speaker and possess no understanding of what goes on in the heads of students, what chance do you have in a classroom?

Then, there is the concept of empathy. If only, there was a class in higher education, which dealt with empathy. Why not require teaching candidates to take an entire semester, perhaps 12 credit hours, of class work that deals with empathy? Without the ability to feel empathy, I think it is impossible to teach.

Christ asked all of humankind to feel empathy. He told a rich man to give everything away, and He spoke of giving one's life for a brother as the highest form of love. He spoke of taking care of widows and orphans, and without question, He was the greatest teacher.

I wonder if we could all do as he asked.

Day 10

Teachers should have serious concerns about the powers of peer pressure. If we look closely at a typical day of school, we see constant influence through interaction. Students come from all walks of life, and the home cultures of each person can differ vastly. Therefore, young people are literally soaked in the outpouring of traits from countless other students. By the end of a day, a person has been touched by the words and actions of so many others that it can sometimes be difficult to hold to personal values, especially for a child who is easily swayed. And some are easily swayed because they are in need of affection or attention, or they need to feel included and might be willing to go to any length to obtain inclusion. It is almost impossible to change a child's home culture through curriculum, but you have a chance if you can reach a child through love and caring and, moreover, through the example you set.

In the end, we can hope to teach them character and set them on a path of self-control and independence, but we know that as we are trying to do this, there is a perpetual scheme working its evil magic to upset our efforts. That scheme is the mob mentality. We must get students to embrace the power of morality and individualism. We must help them think highly of themselves and never be followers. This, of course, is easier said than done, but through prayer and inner strength, a teacher can have a profound influence on young people by talking about morals and serving as a living sacrifice to God. In fact, students notice in a hurry any teacher who appears or talks as if he or she loves God and wants to lead by Christian example. Never forget that peer pressure is perhaps the most dangerous obstacle for children. It might be for adults as well, but at least adults have a greater latitude to resist. Children do not.

May God assert positive peer pressure on children. May God strengthen educators to teach morality and never shy away from it because society says we cannot.

Day 11

I recall feeling as if teachers were unimpressed by me. I believed with all the mistakes I made, no one would let me have another chance to right my wrongs. It seemed that I felt feeble because I was painfully dysfunctional. Of course, that was not something they knew, because I never spoke of it. However, I do vividly recall never having a relationship with any teacher in any way, shape, or form. In fact, I cannot recall a teacher asking me about my life in any facet. There were no questions about needs, wants, dreams, and pains, and I do not remember hearing a single compliment or praise from a teacher, coach, or administrator.

Now that I look back over the long years that have passed, I realize I am responsible for the choices I have made, and it is silly to whine about childhood recollections. It does, however, give me cause to think about what we as educators owe students each and every day of their lives. Bear in mind that school can be a venerable wilderness and children need to hear kind words and praises from adults. If they venture through each day just trying to survive, then sooner or later they will seek out edification from someone, and that could lead to a dysfunctional choice.

There is not a person in the world who does not enjoy hearing a kind word or praise. We all need it. It is as essential as food and water. It should be at the core of teaching. I have watched good teachers, and they are masters at breaking down a child through definition of weaknesses and then building up that child through his or her strengths. This process can sometimes require hard discipline, but master teachers end up molding people in such a way as to polish them and hand over the gift of confidence. Ultimately, we are responsible for our choices, and once we are adults, there is no one to blame but ourselves. But could we have had a better opinion of ourselves if someone had pointed out our beauties and strengths?

Scripture is replete with lessons about life, but there may be no greater that how Jesus dealt with a woman who was about to be stoned to death for adultery. The Jewish religious leaders, who were cold and callused toward the common person thought that they could catch Jesus siding with a sinner, so they tested Him. They said to him, "Teacher, this woman has been caught in the act of adultery. Now in the Law, Moses commanded us to stone such women. So what do you say?" (John 8:4) Jesus said, "Let him who is without sin among you be the first to throw a stone at her." The older ones began leaving one by one, knowing that none was without sin. Jesus stood up and said to her, "Woman, where are they? Has no one condemned you?" She said, "No one, Lord." And

Jesus said, "Neither do I condemn you; **go, and from now on sin no more**."[2] (John 8:5-11)[3] He declared her clean and gave her a chance to start over. We should let children start over every day.[4]

---

[2] **CPH**: Since "there is no man [nor woman] who does not sin" (2 Chron. 6:36) at this time, we cannot go without sinning. In the Scriptures, often "sin" and "sinners" is used to refer to living in sin, or those who have a reputation as sinners. Jesus was not expecting this woman to sin literally **no more**, but rather to no longer live a life of sin as an adulterer.

[3] **CPH**: Later manuscripts add the story of the adulterous woman, numbering it as John 7:53-8:11. In other words, these 12 verses are not found in the earliest and best manuscripts and was certainly not an original part of the Gospel of John; one significant group of Greek manuscripts places it after Luke 21:38, supporting the conclusion that it is a spurious and uninspired text. They have obviously been added to the original text of John's Gospel. It is tradition that keeps them in our English translations.

[4] **CPH**: This is not advocating that we do not discipline our children for more than a day. The punishment may very well be the loss of a cellphone for a week or more. What we do not want to do is go to bed angry with our children. We need to let them know that we love them before the sun sets that evening.

Day 12

All through my career, I have heard the words *special education* or *at-risk student*. I have watched intently as children develop habits and trends in early years that see no corrective action, and then when high school arrives, they fall into a chasm and vanish as dropouts. In fact, I predicted this with several students when I directed the alternative school in our district. I was amazed these kids even made it to school. Some were from homes so dysfunctional that food was a scarce commodity, which in our culture seems impossible. Those students lived in homes with no boundaries and with parents or guardians who found no merit in education. Bad habits can be learned young, and it becomes virtually impossible to change those habits when that student reaches high school. It is only through life's difficulties that some people are able to change.

Schools owe it to society to take seriously the concept of people being at-risk and not simply casting the terminology aside as if it were a meaningless idea that really only applies to seriously handicapped or mentally impaired people. There are emotionally disturbed children in this building who are not identified, and they develop painful problems in silence that are multiplied exponentially through the structure of school.

I keep harping on the ideology of empathy. Empathetic teachers see at-risk students clearly, but interventions are not easily put in place. This creates issues for those students. Perhaps we owe it to students and each other to explore inventive ways to reach those seemingly unreachable children. Sometimes I struggle for answers. My best plans meet with obstacles, but this does not mean I give up. My visions are still accurate even if solutions are elusive.

May God give us the wisdom to create alternative environments and means to reach the unreachable. My prayer today is for the tools and intellect to somehow save the children that can barely function in this building. Lord help us all.

Day 13

Admitting fault or offering an apology is the most important characteristic of a Christian. It is amazing that it is overlooked in favor of other aspects. However, make no mistake, Christ repeatedly asked us to admit our wrongs. It's called repentance, and when we open up our lives to others through humility, we become stronger spiritually.

Throughout my career, I have made countless mistakes — some, in fact, that haunt me still — and I did not always apologize, especially when I was younger and less mature. Now that I have life experience through raising children and being an educator, I have learned that it is a cleansing feeling to say I am sorry, and I have also noticed people I deal with feel my equal, and there is nothing wrong with that even though I may be in charge as building leader. Scripture states that Christ came to this world and made Himself nothing. In other words, He gave up Himself for us. Imagine if every person had that philosophy. How much better the world would be!

It begins in school. It really does. We have the chance to teach humility every day. Children learn from listening to us and watching us, and they do indeed watch everything we do. I believe each of us should say we are sorry about something every day. We make mistakes every day! Of course, we do! Once we admit this, we should let someone know that we feel remorse and need it to be acknowledged. If children witness this firsthand, they begin to understand what it means to care about another person and moreover to be humble.

I pray that we all are able to apologize. Admitting our wrongs to

God is easy. Admitting it to each other is the real test of our souls.

Day 14

Christ never took anything personally unless He was defending the honor of God. But as far as Himself personally, He never was angry over anything anyone did to Him or said to Him. He simply took whatever people dished out and displayed an otherworldly tolerance for the weaknesses of mankind.

Imagine you are in the crowd as soldiers toss insults at Him, whip Him brutally, and spit on Him, and it seems to go on and on. In spite of what He endured, He had the ultimate love by asking God to forgive them because they did not know what they were doing. He lived his life in utter sacrifice, even for the blunders of and evils of others. Children commit evils and blunders literally daily. I wonder if we can teach them without taking these actions personally. Yes, they lie, and yes, they bully, and yes, they steal, and yes, they cheat. We must take them as human and make every attempt to save their lives. I understand that deviance sometimes requires that we fight. I understand that sometimes we can display righteous anger. More often, though, is the propensity human beings have to just be human, and that requires that we display the same deep humility Christ displayed even when He was hanging on nails.

We can ask God to forgive children because they do not know what they are doing.

Day 15

There is a pressing thought on my mind today. Last night as I drove back from a volleyball game, I found myself thinking long about what it means to be a giver. People struggle with this concept more than any other aspect of the human condition. I think the very nature of evil is selfishness. In fact, I am certain it is the terminal disease of the soul. It is not until we become givers that we are truly set free from the world and realize the essence of God.

When I was a child, I would hear people talk about God as if He were available for a phone call as if He was in the next room, and it seemed to me it was easy for people to believe God was a person similar to a counselor or friend. I viewed God as a distant entity, a benevolent Creator who could be reached if I was able to become Christlike. Then and only then was I convinced I could be near God or, moreover, have God live in me daily. It's not enough to believe. I have never bought into the ideology that faith is enough. If we love, we commit, and if we commit, we sacrifice. It is simple. Teaching requires that we give ourselves away to people. It requires that we eliminate selfishness from our minds. It is impossible to care about someone if our first thought is to ourselves.

We should give for the sheer joy of it. Give love, give effort, give compliments, and give knowledge. If we hold something dear, we should hand it over to the human race.

May God give us the power to give it all away.

Day 16

Is it possible to teach creation in a public school? This morning I thought how beautiful it was, with autumn-like temperatures and clear skies. I have always been attached to nature. It is inherent to my being. I sometimes find myself talking to God in the forest or at the river, and it seems I hear clearer replies out there, as opposed to what I think I hear when I pray in a hurry in my vehicle or office. It is creation that I give thanks for today. But in this modern culture that advocates science and either downplays or eradicates the concept of creation, it has become increasingly difficult for a Christian teacher in a public school to speak of creation, much less integrate it into curriculum. However, there is a way.

I am convinced we can teach critical thinking skills by asking students to express how they think the world came into being. I am not advocating a debate between science and religion. Nevertheless, at the core of critical thinking is the concept that science simply does not answer all of the questions, and faith in a higher power is perfectly acceptable to talk about. Teachers can keep discussions in context and allow the expression of students to take place. Where this will lead is an outstanding opportunity to have students ask the teachers for their viewpoint. From there, teachers can open up their hearts to speaking about creation. It's hard these days to blend science and faith, but it can be done and should be done.

I like to tell students that God is the greatest scientist of all. The mysteries of science truly amaze me, and surely it is what we discover through education that clearly reveals God to us. After all, the world is too complex to have been accidental, and it is through exploration that we find truth and, of course, truth and God are synonymous.

Day 17

A child should never have to choose dishonesty for security. A lie should never appear to be a better choice than the truth. When children make mistakes or bad choices, we should create an atmosphere that allows them to arrive at a point of accountability through their own admission. Sometimes we are so intent on finding out the truth and wanting punitive reconciliation that we cause fear to override a child's ability to want the truth instead. We have to teach children that truth is noble and honorable and we will have great respect for them if they choose the truth over a lie.

I once had a teacher enter my office in anger, insisting she had been lied to by a student, and she wanted me to interrogate the young lady and get her to admit her wrongdoing and also get her to admit she lied. The teacher was brooding and forceful, at times intimidating to the student. I watched as she battered the girl with judgment, and finally, the student began to weep. I asked the teacher to leave me with the student temporarily, and in moments through subtle words, I had the young lady admit she lied, and I simply told her I understood.

Sometimes an adult, through pride and anger, can cause a child to choose a lie as opposed to the truth. And why not? Any child, given a choice between being battered by an adult until they are not only punished but also stripped of dignity or telling the truth, is likely to lie. I have seen it so many times that I would state without reservation that 90 percent of children will choose a lie out of fear. Fear should never be a reason to lie, but because people are judgmental, we can create dishonesty. Teachers should foster relationships with students that are based on integrity and honor and, most of all, an environment that is void of fear. Children are more likely to reach for truth than lies if they know they will be treated with respect even in their moments of weakness and error.

Day 18

A life is sometimes measured in a moment. We can work our entire lives for a goal, and the prize will arrive for a few fleeting seconds. This could be an athletic moment of heroism or a man or woman climbing to the summit of Mount Everest to have a view from the top of the world that lasts minutes. Anyone who has ever worked so hard at an endeavor for a moment's exhilaration understands it was all worth it.

And then there are people whose lives are measured in outcomes, such as a degree or perhaps the building of a business. I think teachers should recognize education is a combination of both. It is the moments that make up the lives of students. However, we should be concerned with the outcome. Teaching is a long-range endeavor. The view is an end result of creating a complete man or woman, but along the way, we should celebrate the amazing moments that take place, the accomplishment of a single test score, an idea, a basket by a child that seldom scores, the smile or laughter of a special needs child who rarely, if ever, shows emotion, the artwork, the music, or just the effort, because sometimes effort is a monumental achievement for a person. If we are to lift others to a higher place, it begins by noting their moments and pointing them toward an outcome. Our lives are a work in progress, a movie worth watching if we will make sure to watch.

Day 19

I believe communication is the single most imperative characteristic of a healthy classroom. Of course, it is vital to a relationship as well. I am confident that most failed marriages or friendships are caused to some degree by a lack of communication. If a person simply strolls through life with an inability to communicate or show emotion, such as affection or edification, then it is safe to say someone else is deprived, and it is not an excuse to blame it on personality traits. If that were the case, then we could all make excuses for why we are moody, angry, or simply not wishing to make another person feel included. If it were a manifestation of personality, then most assuredly one should not teach or even get married.

What I mean is that if any of us enter into an agreement that we will help others in any capacity, then we must comprehend the responsibility we have to communicate. Communication means saying, "I love you," showing it, crying for other people, telling them you appreciate them, speaking of their strengths, and showing them they can realize dreams. In reality, communication is opening your heart and mind so others can see into it. Teaching is much like being married. You agreed or even passionately desired to be a teacher, and now that you have entered the union, you should give all of yourself to the journey and polish the emotional and intellectual skills it takes to build a friendship until those who come in contact with you are made better.

Day 20

Today I noticed he had brown eyes. I have seen and dealt with this student countless times already this school year, mostly in negative situations, and we have begun an intervention program for him, and all the while I simply viewed him as a challenge, perhaps a person who needed help. But today I saw that he has brown eyes and a smile, and today he became a soul that is worth our lives to save.

A teacher, a coach, a man, has decided to see who this child really is and took him for a haircut. When the hair was cut away, I could see his face and his eyes for the very first time. I am not sure what this means. It could be that I was not looking closely enough. It could have meant that I saw him purely in superficial aspects. But now I see him as a person who needed someone to take him by the hand and lead him down a different path. I am not naïve enough to think all of our problems have vanished because of a kind gesture and a haircut, but I am most assuredly confident to have discovered just how powerful one kind gesture really is. I spoke briefly with the little brown-eyed boy, and the sudden attention is rather bruising to his dignity. It could be that he realized people may have felt sorry for him, and he finds that embarrassing. I have the thought just now that it's time to cease the pity for him and empower him through love. A man took him for a haircut and helped me to see a child's face for the first time. I think a prayer may have been answered this morning.

Day 21

I once heard it said in a movie that life is not worth living without dreams. Is there really a single person who has never dreamed of something greater than ordinary? I am reminded of movies I have watched in which dreams came to be through struggle, strife, and hard work.

Rudy tried for years to become a Notre Dame football player and ultimately worked on the scout team until his destiny was sealed through the unselfishness of his teammates, and he played a handful of seconds. He waited forever for those precious seconds, but it was a dream realized. Rocky took a shot at the heavyweight title of the world, and all he really wanted was to go the distance. In the waning moments of that movie, I found myself emotional over the idea that a man could suffer so much to lose and yet call it a win. In The King's Speech, a movie I have said was the most important motion picture I have ever seen and a work of art, the teacher, an ordinary man with little or no resume to speak of, took a man of royalty with a speech impediment and lifted him to a higher place for a single speech that may have motivated the British people to endure a darkness that threatened humanity.

When I watched those movies, I realized that dreams truly are the nourishment of the imagination and soul. We want our lives to count for something. We want our lives to have meaning. Today, as you look at the children, we have been charged to lead, remember that they all have a dream, even if they never reveal that dream, and then close your eyes and imagine how rich their lives will be if those dreams are made real. God gives us all the power to dream and the power to choose the labor that could lead us to that dream. I say we have a responsibility to create dreamers.

Day 22

What is curriculum? I mean, really, when all is said and done, what is the meaning of the word? We use it so often as if school could not really function without it. Curriculum is what we teach — literally. I realize it is vital because, of course, we as an institution of learning, charged with preparing people for life in our society, must take seriously what we teach. But perhaps we are not emphasizing what is imperative to the lives of students. In other words, do we sacrifice what is imperative in favor of what is academic?

Let me delve deeper into this. Which is more important, teaching a student about the causes of World War II or teaching the student critical-thinking skills? Is it more important to teach a student how to create a science experiment, or is it more important to teach the skill of articulation? In other words, is it more important to be academic, or is it more important to be empowered? I think even Christ focused on the simple imperativeness of empowerment through His teachings. We sometimes forget that the words in a book are not nearly as important as what we can discern from the book. We are better educators if we can give children the following:

A. confidence;

B. critical thinking skills;

C. a sense of self-worth;

D. freedom to love who they are and who they can become.

These aspects may seem simple or even trivial to some, but in the grand scheme, we are successful if we create strong, empowered, confident, self-controlled, diligent, focused, moral people. In the end, our society is a grander place if we create these people through our curriculum. Do not think I am saying our curriculum is unimportant. What I am saying is that it is secondary to the psychology of those we are teaching. If the soul is greater than the body according to Christ, then most assuredly it applies to our students. Remember that our curriculum only becomes pertinent when we first shape the person.

Day 23

Are the physical experiences of life more important than intellectual realization? Can we teach children that our minds can truly give us greater physical experiences in our lives? I believe that self-realization, the arrival at personal truths, the discovery of the soul and its power, is the greatest revelation of the human condition.

That said, we are obligated as educators to teach children that it is their intellect that gives them hope and vision for who and what they can become. We pay far too much attention to physical accomplishments, such as athletics. I have been involved in sports my entire life and love competition, but make no mistake, I have developed an aching need for intellectual stimulation and a desire to be a lifelong learner. I consider my greatest personal accomplishments to be my education and any aspect of my life that has evolved from that education.

Realization is a deeply profound aspect of the human soul, and it cannot simply be attained through physical experience alone, though I am confident there are moments in our lives that lift us to a place where personal realization is felt in that manner. I have felt this through love, nature, witnessing childbirth, and yes, sometimes in an athletic event. However, to truly feel complete requires that we be spiritual, and that is so much deeper than the raw experience. Let us help students to attain personal realization. Let us help them become thinkers, and then the physical experience becomes something amazing. Teach them that it is through intellect that we become greater. Christ taught spiritual concepts and ideas, always focusing on the soul, always focusing on honing the mind.

Day 24

Think about what makes a person a friend. Think about what is the most powerful trait of a friend. Why do you love or like someone? The reasons might vary, but if you think long about this, you may come to the realization that it is loyalty we seek in people. We all need loyalty. We need to know someone has our back, that someone will stand up for us, that someone will always be there in spite of the coldness of the world and the obstacles we all face, and that, even when we are wrong, they will share in the pain and maybe even die on a hill with us. Perhaps it is the most difficult human characteristic to find among our friends and peers.

I believe loyalty is the sign of a powerful soul, a powerful mind, and the evidence of a godly person. I am not insinuating that people loyal to a bad cause are godly. I am saying that people who understand and possess empathy and, moreover, are able to stand in front of the storm for a friend are the people who are godly.

If you ponder the disciples of Christ and recognize their fears for standing up for Him, then most assuredly you can see how hard it is to be loyal and why it is so amazing when we find loyalty among mortals. Peter denied Christ. Judas handed him over to the mob. Some doubted, and some hid. All of them were afraid. In the end, He died alone. It was not until afterward that they decided to become martyrs.

I once heard it said that uncompromising men are easy to admire but hard to follow. It could be that people are inherently weak, and the weakness is more evident when loyalty is called into question. Children learn bad habits through societal norms. We should teach children to stand up for righteous causes, to take their own word seriously when they give it. Ultimately, we should teach them that courage is beautiful and even more so when we are eager to take the problems of others onto our own shoulders.

Day 25

Today I ponder the pain of dealing with a lost child. This could be any number of students in our school. It could be for any number of reasons as well. There are children here who were lost at birth in families so dysfunctional that moments of contentment are nonexistent. Some children have such severe handicaps that getting them to simply eat or walk through the building without incident is truly an accomplishment. Some children wear filthy clothes for several days and others who cannot wait for our institutional lunch because it is the best food they will see in a day. Some children say hello to me with a smile because they need someone in their lives to communicate with. This description could become endless because problems are endless — so many issues with so many children that it becomes difficult to have faith in a positive outcome.

Have you heard it said that you cannot save them all? I heard a teacher once state that trying to save everyone will drive you crazy, so simply do what you can and do not let it keep you awake at night. I do not share that opinion. I believe we are obligated to try to save all of them. I am certain it is a moral obligation. I am reminded of Christ in the garden, praying as the hour of His death drew nearer and the weight of humanity on His shoulders, of course literally. Somehow, we as educators have to take on the weight of humanity when we look into the eyes of these children. To look at them and discard their problems as too much to deal with is criminal. We must do what we can and then some. Never give up the fight to save every last person. It is the greatest cause on earth.

Day 26

I thought saying the prayer aloud at a football game might invite controversy. I was wrong. People want us to stand up for spiritual living. Football games are a monumental event at our school, especially after winning back-to-back state championships and consistently producing successful student athletes. It was two years ago that I decided we would no longer simply offer a place for people to go gather and say a prayer away from the crowd. I opted instead to ask a local pastor to take the microphone and give the prayer for all to hear. Some in our administration and on our school board were skeptical, but I stated that if we were called on it through some legal channel, then we would reconsider or stop altogether, but people wanted it. Gradually over the past two seasons, we have received compliments for offering what was termed by one man as an old-fashioned approach to school. Yes, there are some aspects of school that change dramatically, and in this technological age, we are required to upgrade, but our moral fiber must stay constant and unwavering even if it is threatened by a society and court system that refuses to reach back to what built this nation and sustained us through trials and tribulations. We were founded on Christian ideologies, and it is those powerful ideas that should lead us. A prayer at a football game is a very strong statement.[5]

---

[5] CPH Blog: Does God Attend Sports Events?

https://christianpublishinghouse.co/2016/12/17/does-god-attend-sports-events/

Day 27

Are we useful or useless? Do our lives reflect the values of a person who gives and not takes? There is a song I like because the poetry and power of the words hit at my core. The words are, "It's all about soul, and under love is a stronger emotion." It is a song by Billy Joel, and each time I hear the words, I am moved by the message. I think useful people, those who are givers and make sacrifices for others and feel such deep and imperative empathy that they take on the problems of other people, are the special ones who realize love is not enough, that under love is truly a stronger emotion, and it's really all about the soul.

Somehow, we must be spiritually strong to the point that we take on the problems of students and that we do so with cheerful and passionate hearts. Think of the child who is in need, and imagine that all you say is, "I love you." It's not enough. It never will be. There has to be something stronger than love, something deeper, and it is an emotion that defies description. I think it is what Christ felt hanging on a Cross to die for others. I think we have to arrive there if we ever hope to comprehend what it means to feel an emotion that is otherworldly. Teaching is the greatest profession, of course. But you cannot be successful in this profession unless you are willing to give up your life for another person, be it the masses or just one child.

Day 28

After much experience and observation, I am convinced that the best teachers are master motivators and possess the ability to raise people to another plane of existence. Think about what inspires us — great people, great speeches, watching someone overcome great adversity to achieve something remarkable — and it is through the strength of others that acquire strength.

Today I watched the video of Gabrielle Andersen Scheiss, the Swiss runner who competed in the 1984 women's Olympic marathon, and I was in tears as she struggled to finish. She had been reduced to a staggering, drunk-like gait until it appeared she might fall. All the while, she fully intended to complete the mission, and as the crowd fell silent, she managed to make it to the finish line. I wept. It was so powerful to observe the human soul overriding the body.

We can literally do anything we set our minds to. God has given us a will to live, a will to fight, and a will to fail. It is what we choose that makes us great. Great teachers believe events and outcomes into being. They imagine success and try to raise others to another level. I am moved by the thought that people in this building are trying to save lives and souls every day, and it is my hope that I can motivate them. Sometimes teachers are expected to work miracles, and with the help of God they really do, but they are also sometimes forgotten by leaders who have expectations for students and not those who are teaching. May God give me the power to motivate these teachers to fight to the finish line.

Day 29

Today I traveled to an education center in eastern Kansas, and I found myself enamored with the technology and facilities of this institution. I particularly liked the observatory and, to a slightly lesser extent, the IMAX-type theater. I felt like a kid as I watched planets rotate and stars blink. It all seemed so close and so real. As I gazed at the infinite power of learning and the vastness of reality, I was struck by the sense that it could not have been an accident. There just had to be a Creator. Something as grand as our universe did not simply come to be by some cosmic stroke of luck, and as I toured the buildings, I found myself in calm humility at the thought of God. The reality is quite simple yet beyond awesome. A single entity formed the most intricate aspects of life and the universe. A single strand of DNA has more evidence of God than all the science through the ages could produce to suggest otherwise. In reality, it is what we learn about ourselves that proves the existence of God, and I am comforted by knowing this. Even the mysteries bring a smile to my face because the exploration that will lead to uncovering those mysteries is just more journeys to realize God. Yes, God and education really do belong together.

Day 30

A child with special needs just read me a story. When he finished, he gave me a high-five slap to the hand, and his smile could have covered the largest field of wildflowers on the planet. The story consisted of about ten pages, with no more than a few words on each page. He had asked to read it to me earlier in the day, and his teachers let me know. It amazes me that so little in the grand scheme could mean so much to a single life. I read books and comprehend what I read. This boy reads perhaps 40 words total in a few minutes, more than likely comprehends little if any, and it is a monumental accomplishment. His face said it all. It was not the words or the accomplishment of reading that gave him the elation. It was the attention he received from me, and my very soul is reenergized by his need. May God always show me the depths of the human soul. And it is my mission, beginning now, to get as many high-five slaps from that little boy that I can throughout this school year.

Day 31

I had a thought last night before bed that sometimes it seems devout Christians are passionate for God, forsaking all else and anyone else. I am not sure how to articulate my thoughts, but at a deep level, this disturbs me, and sometimes it's hard for me to express why. I think we were put on this planet to be relational and to love one another. Somehow, through the trials and tribulations of life, we gradually gravitate toward a need for God. I think it is inevitable that we will search for God. It is something innate to our being. But some people find God, have faith in God, and ultimately love God to the point that their lives are so heavenly focused they become of no earthly good.

There is a reason why more than half of all Christian marriages end in divorce. I believe it is because those people develop trust and love for God but offer nothing to the spouse. In other words, they cannot give the same deep commitment to a mortal that they give to God. I think this is a sad trait of people who really do not have the deep relationship with God they thought they might have had. To love God, we must give our lives away to others in this world. We are here to live and discover God, and the only way to discover God is through what we learn about each other and what we give to each other. There is a deeper mystery in all of this. It's hard to articulate, as I already stated. But the very essence of life is love and sacrifice, or something even deeper, and it is those people who discover the mystery who really find themselves in the vicinity of God. If we learn this at a young age, we live it as we get older. Children must feel the power of God through our words and actions. We cannot allow our focus on God to be blinding to reality.

Day 32

I am reminded today that leadership is effective only if it is sacrificial. Christ was a leader, although we often do not look upon Him as so. We tend to equate leadership with power, and therefore it is hard to visualize Christ being powerful when He advocated meekness and humility. I believe leadership is powerful when it is gentle, edifying, intellectual, loving, kind, and, moreover, morally strong. A man or woman can be an effective leader through moral traits and still be able to handle a crisis or make a tough decision.

People followed Christ even to the death in some cases. If Christ advocated turning the other cheek, then surely He resented aggression and macho power displays. I would almost assure any person seeking to become a leader that people follow who they respect and despise who they are intimidated by. It would have been impossible to fear Christ. It would have been impossible to term Him as intimidating. He was, in fact, a persuasive teacher, an articulate philosopher, and a loving commander. How did He manage such a paradoxical state of being? How can any of us be commanders and yet in the same breath be loving? I think it is accomplished only through the most profound meditation and prayer. I think truly great leaders possess amazing empathy, a word I keep revisiting because it is so imperative. And to be in possession of great empathy requires a gentle spirit. I would like to believe I would and could follow Christ anywhere, but that requires courage I do not always possess. May God give me that courage. I can only hope that through my actions people see me as a leader and not because of my secular strength but because of my spiritual power is drawn from the example of Christ.

Day 33

Can we as educators view the mistakes children make as opportunities for learning? I cannot help but notice at times how adults tend to view the mistakes of youths as intentional and worthy of chastisement. I have come to realize that a person can either make a mistake or a bad intention, and there is a clear difference. A mistake is a blunder in the midst of life. A bad intention is something entirely different. A bad intention is rooted in evil. It is easy to discern the difference, and once that is done, we can easily understand that children need to be allowed to make mistakes in their quest to determine the truth. As educators, we owe it to them to use a mistake as an opportunity to grow and improve. As I think back on life, I can see so many mistakes that I made. In fact, I sometimes am haunted by the list. But thankfully, those mistakes made me better. My bad intentions, however, were a darkness I needed to be released from, and it is during those times that I needed discipline. God disciplines those He loves, and none of us should shun discipline. We as educators should practice discernment and help children know right from wrong as well as how to seek the truth through errors.

Day 34

This morning I feel confronted by spiritual issues, and I cannot really ascertain what they are — not clearly anyway. I am wondering if God is at work in all things. I see so much conflict in the lives of people, and my heart aches for ways to help, but I am limited because I am mortal. I cannot take the place of God in their lives. If they do not seek God for comfort and strength, then my limitations are all the more evident. I do, however, love and love completely. That has to be enough. It has to be enough that I possess empathy and feel the pain that burdens others. If an educator can come to a school every day and not notice the immense burdens children carry, then surely they do not possess empathy. I can most surely be a role model to these students. I owe it to them to be an example. May God empower me to do so. I will pray today as I walk into the building. It is not just for the children but also for me. I need God and want God in my life. I am powerless on my own to defeat the demons that rip at the souls of these children and fight for ownership of them eternally. If I could live or die for others, I would. May God reveal my destiny in prayers that I speak each day and the hopes that I have.

Day 35

Each of us has personal issues and obstacles in our lives from time to time, some more so than others. Do we realize our jobs as educators are a professional and moral obligation that requires us to rise above our personal dilemmas so we can focus on children? This requires us to have powerful self-discipline or self-control, a personal inner force that gives each of us the strength daily to persevere so we can pay attention to pressing moral concerns in education. In my experience, I have witnessed a wide array of personal issues in the lives of teachers, such as divorce, bankruptcy, personal loss, and even life-threatening diseases. Any of those dreadful aspects of life can be painfully distracting, in fact debilitating, and it is difficult to hold the line, so to speak, and come to work each day with one's eyes trained on the mission. Somehow, we must hold the line. Can teachers realize that pushing education to the forefront of human lives is mission work? Can teachers realize that without education and positive moral influence, a child will be lost in a vicious world? I think an educator must spiritually train, much like a fighter who runs daily and punches a bag until he or she is exhausted. Without self-discipline and the power of a focused soul, no man or woman has a chance against the darkness that encroaches daily in the lives of us all. I am not sure how to train a soul, but I feel confident it begins with meditation. Educators must find time to think, pray, and reason. If this means developing an exercise routine, walking each evening, reading, or sitting alone in a beautiful setting, then it must take place. What is at stake is profound.

Day 36

What is important? I mean really, when all is said and done, what is important in this world? I had a thought last night that perhaps what we think is important is probably not important to God. What I mean is the trivial aspects of life such as status, the outcomes of contests, the day-to-day petty drama, and what type of car we drive or the house we live in are just not going to get the attention of the Creator of the universe. With all the problems going on in this world, such as famine, disease, war, hatred, and the list goes on and on, an all-powerful, benevolent God is more than likely not concerned about the homecoming court, the final score, or who is leading the vote on Dancing with the Stars. We must reach the children in this building and teach them what is important. Are we asking our students to become those next generation people who discover the cure for all cancers or devise a way to feed the starving people of Third-World nations, or become ambassadors that stamp out hatred and war, or build an economy that sustains all people and not just those who can afford a better life? Or will they be kind people who extend a helping hand to those who are in need of relationships? We have a moral obligation to teach them what is important.

Day 37

Children must believe school is relevant. An adult, of course, knows an education is vital, but children simply cannot comprehend that life and quality of life are dependent upon knowledge. I am a believer in constructivism as an approach to learning. I feel certain we learn naturally if our ideas meet up with experiences. In other words, this is similar to the concept of hands-on learning. A person cannot know God by simply attending church, singing, partaking of a ceremony, or reading. A person knows God through experiencing God, and that means fellowship, humanitarianism, prayer, etc. If children are to learn, then surely we as educators need to offer them experience through education connected with their own ideas, and then we can polish that person into an independent, critical thinker. Simply sitting at a desk listening to a person lecture or working on an assignment with no human interaction will not lead to a polished person. It might lead to the same kind of person who attends church and listens to a pastor and leaves. That person ultimately might stop attending church. See the similarity? A person usually quits something because he or she sees it as irrelevant.

Day 38

A public school can be a vicious place for a child. School, in fact, is a wilderness in so many ways. A child arrives at an early hour, and for the remainder of a long day, he or she is subjected to the views, opinions, sorrows, and cruelties of so many other children that we should not be surprised that a child would want to avoid coming to school. A counselor I once knew said that for some children, school is a bad place, and moreover, some children just do not belong in school. She was right to say this. I have long since thought the same thing based on my observations of children being ripped apart by words and gestures. Even the structure of school can sometimes be too much for a child. And, of course, teachers are sometimes guilty of contributing to the madness.

A properly operated school is a safe haven. I tell people that every child should be able to attend school daily and feel safe from the words and gestures that can be toxic. I realize, of course, that I am speaking of a portion of the population. Some children have great experiences in school. But let us be mindful of those who are afraid in this building. When I arise from bed in the mornings and come here, I am continuously reminded that the building is only as safe as I am willing to make it. I have a duty to build spiritual fences around children and teachers to keep out the unkind forces that want in.

Day 39

This morning, the little boy in the wheelchair smiled broadly at me and said hello. The little boy with special needs laughed at something said by another special needs student. One little boy in this same classroom was singing, and I thought perhaps he might as well have been singing to God because we could not understand him, but he appeared happy.

A little girl passed by me in the hallway and stared at the floor as she walked. I thought I saw her doing the same yesterday, and I wondered if she was sad. I learned this morning that two boys in our school lost their home to fire last night. I learned about an hour ago that an employee was angry because she felt slighted by poor administration. A parent called yesterday complaining about a teacher, and I received an email from a parent last night that simply brimmed over with negativity. A woman complained about the crossing guard yesterday, so I watched today, and the two fellows working the crossing are great guys and work hard at it. I can only shake my head at the thought of people always needing drama or something to gripe about.

In the midst of negativity, I am reminded that our faculty is the best in this district and care so much about children that it is hard for me to produce a negative word about any of them. In fact, I cannot. People who have bad experiences in school tend to think their own children are having negative experiences when, in fact, they are not. It is that much more imperative that we as educators build a relationship with parents to take away their fears. We owe it to them to exhibit a culture of godliness.

Day 40

I think this is the meaning of life. We must give all of ourselves to God and people, or even at the very slightest, we must not give kindling to the fire of selfishness. Each day is a chance to be sacrificial, and to miss the day and the chance is to allow another person to hurt or be lost. We cannot take lightly our obligations to one another. So many people walk or run through life, passing by opportunities for commitment. I am afraid that people who cannot make a commitment to God or another person and back it up with passion simply do not understand the essence of Christ. And you cannot be committed to God and leave out people from this formula. Christ did not leave us out.

Yes, I am sure the meaning of life is giving and giving deeply of ourselves to God and others. People who cannot commit to God or a friend or cannot stay tuned into the needs and wants of a spouse, or pick up a hurt stranger, or just give for the simplistic joy of giving, are missing the ultimate responsibility of a Christian. And yes, a Christian is responsible. Believing is not enough. It never will be. We must act on our love and commitment. We must live our lives as if running a race, just as Paul stated during his plight. And with this being established at a personal level, an educator would, of course, realize that so many children need this commitment from us.

Day 41

Today I had the opportunity to observe our seventh-grade students in a relaxed setting. It's amazing what a person can see when children are not in a confined area and are allowed to move about and interact. Our courtyard is large enough to allow the students the flexibility to create space, and I began to notice how certain students gravitate toward one another and leave others isolated. In addition, I noticed that the old clichés like cliques and peer groups are indeed very true. Without our guidance, children will sometimes behave like wild animals. I realize that is a harsh analogy, but it is true in my view. In fact, there are times when people treat each other far worse than some species of animals. Today, the popular students gradually ended up as an island some 50 yards away from the remainder of the seventh grade. There was another group slightly larger that clustered together, and then there were multitudes of small groups, as few as three to a group, and finally there were two students walking alone in the corners of the courtyard. I watched closely, and other students did not notice. They were caught up in the freedom of visiting, and I realize they simply do not always comprehend the pain that is caused by isolation. I am not sure how to solve this, but I do think we as adults must be vigilant, watch for the isolated children, and somehow bring them closer to others.

Day 42

A friend of mine was chastised by her boss today and left the office in tears. She was shattered. She is a kind and decent person with godly intentions. In fact, I could work for her if she were the leader of our school. A simple moment of disagreement led to a near catastrophic encounter that ultimately led to hurt feelings and, in the end, it is difficult to imagine she will ever feel totally loyal to the person she answers to. I wonder if we truly understand how to lead like Christ. Could we really be strong in our meekness? Could we lead others by example and never display pride or arrogance? Could we realize that empathy is at the core of success and that giving of ourselves is perhaps the hardest thing of all but ultimately the supreme indicator of Christian enlightenment? I can only hope that somehow teachers see Christ in me. I can only hope my leadership is powerfully gentle and humble.

Day 43

On Saturday, I was paused in an intersection in Hays, Kansas. I noticed a man on a bicycle waiting for the light to change so he could cross. He had Down syndrome. I am not sure why, but it struck me at that moment that the world is filled with lonely people, and I wondered if he was lonely. He waited patiently for the light to change, but by then I had driven on.

If you have ever been to Hays, Kansas, you will know that the western Kansas sky is huge and the landscape goes on eternally. It seems much like an ocean of grass. You must like wide-open spaces and solitude to find joy in Hays, Kansas. The thought of him waiting for the light to change in a place so isolated from the rest of the country made me think more of loneliness as an individual plight or contemplative existence. Some people suffer being alone, while others seem to need it.

Imagine you are waking up this morning, and you are alone in your home. Everyone you love is gone. Today you will go to work, go to the grocery store, come back home, eat dinner, and go to bed again, and all alone. There is no one to say goodbye as you leave the house and no one to greet you when you return. Imagine that this goes on for years. Now imagine it is that way every day for some child in our school. The intersections of our hallways are full of people that drive by. They are all headed somewhere but only pay you a glance. They have friends of their own and do not stop to speak to you. This is much like that man in the intersection in Hays.

Perhaps my analogy is not painting a good picture for you because you struggle to relate to loneliness. Perhaps you would not have felt the same had you been sitting in that intersection in Hays and saw him. I only know how it made me feel. I wanted to stop and say hello. I wondered where he was going with his bag of groceries hanging from his handlebars. I wondered if he had someone waiting for him somewhere. I think we should start assuming that all of our students are lonely. I think we should start watching the intersections of our hallways.

Day 44

I am not an advocate of school elections. I am not an advocate of student councils, particularly at the middle-school level. Really, all we are talking about is an organized popularity contest. In my observations, I have learned that children are incapable of casting votes for other children to establish who is best equipped to head up an organization. In fact, adults can barely pull it off through our political parties, and conflicts arise between conservatives and liberals. Why should we think that children who can scarcely take serious the need to brush their teeth are really going to be able to create and facilitate a fair election based on character and skill? When all is said and done, they end up voting for popular kids, athletic kids, or a host of other ridiculous reasons. The end result is inequity and the fostering of ill feelings and bad school experiences.

As educators, we owe it to children to teach them equity and set up ways for all of them to succeed and flourish in the school culture. We should do away with beauty contests, class elections, and any other traditional methods for trying to teach what we, as adults cannot seem to do well either. If Americans vote for whoever is going to pad their wallets and set up the best economy despite having any sense of morality, then are we really going to allow students to conduct elections based on equally silly reasons? We have an obligation to teach morals, and equality is in that curriculum. The prettiest, strongest, or best-dressed student seems to win in school, and surely, given our level of intellect and desire to teach children to create a better world, we could pull off something more cultured than a class election based on placing money in a jar or which student can promise luxuries. Think about it. The student council is nothing more than our popular students, and we really cannot come up with any valid reasons those students were elected other than their status with peers. Is this fostering anything other than the assuredness that our students will look at our own elections in the same light?

Day 45

There was a moment this morning when I reflected on a single statement made by a coach to me so long ago. I was intent upon pleasing him, and when I asked if he wanted coffee from the break room, he turned and delivered an obscenity my way and laughed as his peers shared in his delight. I was embarrassed and humiliated. That was more than two decades ago. I was a young man trying to make it as a fledgling educator, and he was an established coach in a college football program.

At that time, I was a volunteer assistant and learning the trade of coaching football in a very successful setting. I left that program for a full-time job a few months after that incident, and I have not spoken to him or seen him since, but make no mistake; I have never forgotten his words or the laughter that followed. It is etched in my mind as if someone had thrown scalding water on my skin. I can see now that I was young and impressionable and desiring to impress my peers and those above me. I wanted sorely to succeed, and I worked hard to serve people and hopefully show I was a team player. To this day I have no idea why the older staff member found me worthy of his chastisement. I did learn the power of my intentions and words. What I say and what I do can have a long-term impact on another life. In fact, it could make or break a person. I sometimes wonder if educators fully realize this. In Scripture, the power of our speech is taken seriously, and God tells us that what comes from our tongues reveals the contents of our hearts.

Day 46

The following passage was written by Portia Nelson, a former singer and actress on Broadway.

I. I walk down the street. There is a deep hole in the sidewalk. I fall in. I am lost . . . I am helpless. It isn't my fault. It takes me forever to find a way out.

II. I walk down the same street. There is a deep hole in the sidewalk. I pretend I don't see it. I fall in again. I can't believe I am in the same place. But it isn't my fault. It still takes a long time to get out.

III. I walk down the same street. There is a deep hole in the sidewalk. I see it is there. I still fall in . . . it's a habit. My eyes are open. I know where I am. It is my fault. I get out immediately.

IV. I walk down the same street. There is a deep hole in the sidewalk. I walk around it.

V. I walk down another street.[6]

I am certain this poem is a lesson in responsibility. Educators owe it to children to teach them to avoid the deep holes, take responsibility for choices, persevere trying to change the course, not make excuses, and ultimately choose better paths. Sometimes our focus on school involves only the academic aspects. Let us focus more on character and godly attributes.

---

[6] Portia Nelson, There's a Hole in My Sidewalk: The Romance of Self-Discovery (Hillsboro, OR: Beyond Words Pub., 2012), 35th ann. edition; http://www.goodreads.com/author/quotes/301895.Portia_Nelson.

Day 47

How should we define empathy? What does it really mean? I asked a group of college students I was lecturing last week for their answers to my questions, and one young woman gave perhaps the defining statement that I have so often used but rarely hear. Empathy, she said, is taking on the burdens of others. I say it is that and more. It is spiritually attempting to become another person. It is the man who understands what it means to be a woman, and then he can see the world through the eyes of his wife. It is the woman who understands what it means to be a man and can see the world through the eyes of her husband. It is the friend who feels the pain of disease suffered by a friend. It is the people walking down the street who see the man at the intersection holding a sign that states, "Will work for food," and their hearts bleed and their minds possess no judgment. It is the teacher who looks at all children and knows where they come from, why they hurt, why they cry, why they are hungry, and why they need attention. That teacher truly gets it, gets the big picture. I cannot overstate the concept of empathy. It is at the core of humanity. A lack of it is the cause of every war and the fertilizer of hatred. The man or woman who possesses empathy has a view of the universe more penetrating than the most powerful telescope, and through that view is God.

Day 48

Do you lead a contemplative life? Some people have no idea what it means even after defined. Do you labor at self-control and self-discipline? Do you suffer anything to better yourself spiritually? I am certain that excess leads to laziness, and a lack of self-control or self-discipline leads to collapse. Teachers should spend every day in meditation and attempt to lead lives that are the model of contemplative existence. This allows for a clearer mind. In fact, being a teacher is a spiritual experience and requires that we focus on the mind and soul. This means we take on the monastic approach to both our personal lives and our professions. You cannot simply view education as a job that requires checking in and checking out at the end of the day, collecting a paycheck, and having our summers off. No indeed! This is a calling. This is a deeply powerful responsibility. I liken it to marriage. It demands that we realize who we are and what is needed of us, and this is best ascertained through the contemplative existence. Tell yourself that today you will pray, and you will have moments of silence filled with deep contemplation. Tell yourself that today is the first day of the rest of your life. Be contemplative.

Day 49

What if each of us committed one random act of kindness per day and kept a personal score? What could be the problem with this? Why is it that people do not share this part of their lives? It could be because we should be doing it anyway and recognition is from God in spirit. I am only proposing that we hold one another accountable for random acts of kindness. It is simply something the world needs more of. Remember the song, "What the world needs now is love, sweet love?" I heard it when I was a child, and it stuck. Yes, it would be hokey if a kid heard us singing it as we walked the halls, but all poetic aspects of life seem hokey to people who cannot express emotion. I think every person should have to read a little poetry in his or her lives. Much of the Bible, particularly the Old Testament, is written poetically. I think as the world has aged, it has become cold and calloused toward the sharing of kindness, the display of emotion, and moreover, the exchange of poetic thoughts. To get close to God requires that we give up pride and relinquish all we are in exchange for complete expressions of kindness and giving. What an amazing culture to create and spread.

Day 50

This morning as I drove to school I heard a song by Karen Carpenter. There was a line in it that went like this.

> So here I am with pockets full of good intentions
> But none of them will comfort me tonight

As a Christian, one must accept the hard truth that in spite of our best intentions, we may not find comfort. The world can be a cold, dark place to kind people. I once heard a man say that evil has a grand scheme, and I believe this to be true. That scheme includes making decent, kind people feel frustrated and hopeless. However, within those feelings, we must find perseverance and willpower. We must fight the good fight and expect it to be uncomfortable. Christ was persecuted for no other reason than being different than the norm of that time. He was kind, decent, loving, understanding, and literally every other form of perfection, and the people of that day and age were threatened by His purity. Any Christian should expect no comfort from a godless culture. Stay the course, and find comfort in discomforting trials. If we are anything like Christ, then we can expect to be treated as different and threatening. Do not be surprised when you experience discomfort in spite of your best intentions.

Day 51

How does a school become a role model for a community? Is this possible? Can a school actually be an institution a community looks to as a moral compass? I would submit to you that a successful school is, in fact, a moral compass, and an unsuccessful school is an immoral compass. A community will sometimes rise and fall according to the bearings received from the education of their own children. Think about it. Parents want better lives for their children for the most part. With that in mind, take into account that children spend more than seven hours a day involved in school through most of the year, either in classrooms, on buses, or at events, and if we totaled all the time spent by children in the school culture, it amounts to so very much time that what they learn from us and how they use it will impact a community at a profound level. To think otherwise makes us naïve. Communities and schools are intertwined, and it is up to teachers to be the building blocks. So at the core of this is a simple question: Are we positive role models for the community? If we are then our school most assuredly is as well. The influence of education is spiritual.

Day 52

If only we understood the impact, we have on each other. Did it ever occur to you that each of us needs the edification of others? The person who cooks and the person who cleans and the people who teach and the people who lead are all really in this together, and not one is greater or lesser than the other. When we realize this, we truly are at our best. I believe daily acts of random kindness need, to begin with recognition of our peers. What better way to build the culture of a school than recognizing the contributions and passion of others you work with. In fact, without it we are spinning our wheels. I sometimes notice that leadership seems to indulge in the need to exercise power over people and only point out negatives. I am not sure why this is, other than the possibility that leaders who lead this way lack empathy. Perhaps it is a harsh reality, but those people who lead this way should not be in a role to lead. Christ was perfect in all ways, and He possessed the ability to make the weakest and most broken man or woman feel new. That feeling can be accomplished through peer support. Can we start now?

Day 53

This is an excerpt from a poem I wrote last year. It is the fragments of a larger poem about the effects of divorce on a child. It is the perspective of two brothers who experienced the divorce of their parents.

> A woman and a man are at divergence, And when finally that partition is built
> He and I are left to gather crumbs from half-eaten bread
> Left on the table,
> By half beaten souls —

I wonder if we realize as educators that so many of our students experience the pain of divorce. It is a real issue with so many. If you consider that half of all marriages end in divorce, then you are able to ascertain that roughly half of the students in our building have watched their parents get divorced. Each of the children in our building that have endured this painful process feel what it is to gather crumbs from half-eaten bread, or in other words, gather what little love remains after a half-lived life is broken. Divorce is only one of many godless issues people are confronted with in our society, and it is imperative that we recognize the needs of our students who live through this. Actually, they never really stop living through it. The long-term effects cannot really be understood other than those obvious residual traits children exhibit. Let us be cognizant today that half of our building is dealing with or has dealt with this process.

Day 54

What is our vision of children? How far into their future can we see? What do we see as they walk by us in hallways or when they interact with us and we exchange words and expressions? Let me tell you what I think I see. The bell rings and classes change. Children scurry about, trying to ready themselves for the next class. In the midst of the foot traffic:

A little girls laughs, and I think, She might be a teacher someday.

That boy could be a doctor.

A pair of girls drop books at the same time, and I think maybe I see two lifelong friends who will never move from this town.

And that little girl could be a senator.

And that little boy might just have the personality to be a news anchor.

That little boy will be in prison.

And she will be abused by a husband she felt forced to marry.

And he will be addicted to alcohol and possess a violent temper that lands him in therapy.

She will wreck her car and die.

He will father a child out of wedlock and leave it forever.

He will be addicted to pornography.

She will have cancer at a young age and die, leaving behind three children.

He will own a business locally.

She will live in Europe because she always wanted to travel.

And he will almost certainly be divorced several times and end up addicted to pharmaceutical drugs.

Perhaps I see too much or simply do not see enough. But we should be thinking that children can turn any way the wind blows unless we play an enormous role in heading them in the right direction. Look closely today. Have the eyes of Christ, and think of how wonderful you wish they would all turn out to be.

Day 55

When I awoke this morning, a steady rain fell through the cold darkness. I had spent the night in thought, occasionally praying for someone I was concerned about. I suppose I am really connected to this ideology of empathy, and sometimes I feel so deeply that it keeps me from being content. Now this is both a good and bad feeling. The good is obvious because compassion means I can also love, but the bad is that I am not turning it over to God in faith.

Let me be your model of what not to do. Do not lie awake tossing and turning, looking at the cold windows of a room, thinking of the pain another might be feeling, and wishing that Santa was real and I could just forward a note to him and everything would turn favorable. Do what I should have done. Pray that God will take over completely and a sovereign power of peace would spread across my soul and speak to me that no matter how it all turns out, love and eternal perfection will be achieved because it is the will of God. For me, that is hard to do. I have, to be honest about it and confront perhaps one of my greatest weaknesses as a man. I want to repair broken lives and events, and although I may have the greatest of intentions, it is not always how God works. Faith means giving up the reins to a powerful force. It means believing. It means believing God can have a grand purpose even when it appears no light is penetrating the dark nights of life. We must feel empathy, of course. However, never forget that God feels empathy beyond anything we can comprehend, and events must take place to perfect us.

Day 56

Yesterday I met two people with differing pains. One was a man who was angry about school, and another was a woman hurt about school. They each voiced their frustrations and pains to me in the parking lot of a local business. The man was the father of a student I suspended many years ago for various serious issues. The woman had attended a football game quite recently and could not get in because she had no money. She suffers from mental illness, and I feel great empathy when I speak with her. She was also emotional because she was not allowed to have her pet in the football facility, and at the level she thinks, that seemed as though she could not bring her best friend with her to the game. The man has suffered from issues with substance abuse, and he viewed his son's suspension as unjust, although the boy took complete responsibility for his actions and was kind to me.

The two people, although different in profound ways, both possess feelings about our school that is more common than we realize. Our school is viewed as the greatest institution in this community, and graduates or even those who drop out have experiences that last a lifetime. We simply cannot assume that everyone thinks our school is a wonderful sanctuary. In reality, to some our school is a source of great regret, pain, remorse, bitterness, and a whole parade of other emotions. Our task as educators is to simply reach out and meet them where they are and extend a warm hand or a kind word or gesture, and perhaps they will see our institution and our intentions in a different light. Empathy means feeling what they feel, even if we do not agree or cannot repair the broken heart.

Day 57

How, in this modern age of political correctness and cynicism, can we educate children and infuse their lives with the hope they will each find God? Our system is no longer Christian-friendly. This is a painful reality. The world has changed dramatically since I was a child. God is no longer a focal point in education. In fact, teachers must be careful in our society not to speak of their personal beliefs in a manner that forces those beliefs on children. In addition to that, our society has gradually become cold to the concept that our country was in fact born through Christian values.

There is no escaping the truth that people seeking religious freedom, Christian freedom, founded our nation. Although I am open-minded to other people believing what they wish, I am not agreeable with the ideology that our nation should be a religious melting pot. This is not an extreme thought process by any stretch. If all religions were at the core of our nation's power, then our nation would soon become a mirror image of whatever those religions are. A mirror image of Christianity is what we were all along, and that core belief made us strong. This is not close-mindedness or discriminatory. It is truth. How to do this in school is simple: the pledge, prayer at football games, teachers being role models, etc. God is really here if that is what we wish for and work for.

Day 58

I was entertained this morning by watching the USC marching band playing with Fleetwood Mac. The band members were clearly having the time of their lives performing alongside such an iconic group. I was struck by the thought that each of those students was doing what made them happy. They were music majors more than likely, and they were playing for people along the road leading to a football stadium. People were about to pay a fortune for tickets to that game because they wanted to watch the athletes perform. The band cost nothing, and I hate to point out that playing one of those instruments takes a talent that defies most athletic-minded people. I am an athlete and have coached, and I wish I could play music. In fact, I regret not learning, but I grew up in a culture that advocated sports — and what a loss for me. If I had it to do over, I would be a drummer or perhaps play the saxophone, but play music I would do, and gladly choose it over some of the negative sports moments I have had. I suppose what I am getting at is that we educators should be pushing the arts more than we do, and in doing so, we would create a culture that did not focus on a specific ability or activity, and students would feel free to go with their talents and not with our societal insensibilities. Of course, godly empathy really allows us to see what a child could be and not where our desires lead them.

Day 59

I think we sometimes are guilty of viewing child abuse as beatings or negligence. Let me offer you a different angle. What about ignorance? I sometimes wonder if parents realize a household held hostage by ignorance is just as detrimental to the future of a child as physical abuse. A person who refuses education and then brings children up to go the same way is painfully responsible for the results. Illiterate people who look upon education as an evil institution seem to pass this sentiment along to their children. I am basing this on countless examples I have personally observed in my career.

So many people see no value in education, and their children watch this example. The result is poor attendance, apathy, and ultimately they become dropouts or at the very least poor performers in the classroom while they are struggling to attend. The parent who advocates education praises the merits of intellectual growth, and persistently advocates literacy creates a better life for a child. I believe there are moral implications. It is irresponsible for parents to neglect the education of children and ultimately take the chance that the child raised without education will develop unethical and immoral tendencies. Think me too harsh to suggest such a concept?

If Christ was intent on teaching mankind to have open eyes and reach for godly knowledge, then how could anyone stop there? A broadened mind is a healthy mind. We must be advocates of education.

Day 60

This morning I readied for another day while watching the sad demise of a major college football program and the dismissal of a coach who had become a college football icon. Only a week ago I prayed to God that I would find the wisdom not to take athletics too seriously and to place it in a proper context. I suppose my concerns stem from the harsh truth that our society has simply gone overboard with a fascination or obsession with sports and those men and women who play on high-profile teams, especially those teams that sell tickets and fill stadiums. In education, we sometimes miss the chance to emphasize intellectualism over physical attributes.

If you think my thought process is off base, then ask yourself this: If the library was short of books and needed more resources, and our football or basketball program needed new jerseys, and we polled the public, how do you think the vote would turn out? I have a pretty good idea, but it would only be my theory. Most people will pay a fortune for a ticket to a football game and contribute literally nothing to the education of their children. Now bear in mind that I love sports, and I am one of those who buys tickets, but in my maturity, I have learned that investing in academics has a better chance of improving the world than investing in sports. If the physical attributes of children were more important than the intellectual, then our world would be barbaric and void of spiritual qualities. But of course, I may have just described the fans in the bleachers at my last college football game.

Day 61

There is an iconographic image of Christ in Saint Catherine's Monastery, located at Mount Sinai, considered the oldest in the world that depicts Christ as teaching or blessing. Obviously, to be a Christian is to believe Christ was the Messiah, the Son of God, but I wonder if we fully grasp the power of Christ as a teacher and what that can mean to us as educators. Yes, His focus was on moral teachings, but further study reveals that Christ was an instructor of life lessons and common sense — that He wanted people to grow and improve, and He continually asked His followers to sacrifice themselves for others. He possessed marvelous patience, and I can visualize Him speaking clearly and calmly, His face kind and inviting as His words echoed higher order. Anyone who knew Him and spent time with Him would have been a follower, learning constantly, and desiring to emulate Him. It is a humbling thought, but we as educators should hope children see Christ in our teaching methods and desire to emulate us.

Day 62

Peter, the disciple, is perhaps best known for denying Christ three times on the evening of His betrayal. All of my life I have read Scripture and Peter seemed to have been the beautiful friend of Christ and an ordinary man who was weak at times, a blubbering mess under pressure, and then ultimately one of the greatest messengers in the history of Christianity. I think this is evidence that we can be flawed and bruised but still be amazing workers for our God and Savior. Sometimes when I am beating up on myself, I am reminded that the saints of old were flawed men. I believe, in fact, that it is the saint that is aware of sin, haunted by it, and always fighting it as an enemy. We as educators must first recognize our weaknesses, and then our strengths are exhibited in manifold colors. Start every day by opening your mind to your weakness and planning how it will be overcome, and let this mindset be your early-morning curriculum. From there you will be a fiercer vessel for God to wage war on the darkness that vows to steal our innocence.

Day 63

In the Confessions of Augustine, he wrote, "Behold my heart's ears are turned to you." It is metaphoric of course, but it really possesses deep meaning. Do our hearts have ears? Can we hear with the soul? What should we be listening for? I pray in quiet places, and it is there I hear words with my heart. This is how I know I am tuned into the vernacular of God. We live in a world of disdain, heartache, and misery, and I do not want to think or believe my God is a God of sorrow. I wish to have faith that my God is a God of hope, of peace, of love, and if we are giving to one another without needing reciprocation, then we truly can hear God with our hearts. I am certain mankind becomes so calloused through life and interaction that our species becomes like wild creatures fighting daily over scraps of meat. It is only through tears that we shed the weight of pain, and it is only through listening with the heart that we hear the purity of God's speech. I love the forest and streams of this region, and it is there I go to find solitude and to speak to God, and it is there I hear clearly. I suggest you find a place where you can go and hear clearly.

Day 64

This is hard to articulate, but perhaps easier to write. I think we owe it to one another to take the blame. I realize that is leaving the door wide open for a whole host of questions, but let me try to break it down to a simple thought process. It seems to me that very few people ever apologize for anything. In fact, I cannot relate the last time I heard an apology uttered from human mouths in a school. Surely there have been mistakes made and milk spilled, so why is it that no one says, "I am sorry"? At some deep level, that is what is wrong with the world and why it is hard for mankind to live a righteous existence.

Imagine if you saw a train wreck and the aftermath was horrific. Would you ask what caused it, or would you simply start helping? Now relate that to our daily lives. Everyday things break and train wrecks happen. Do you spend time trying to locate the cause to blame someone, or are you busy being the solution? If we as Christians are busy taking on the problems and train wrecks of others, then we most assuredly are helping with the solutions.

I have a personal routine. Every day I attempt to be accountable for as much as I can. Sometimes I am accused by those closest to me of being a doormat or one of those people who says I am sorry for everything. I suppose that stems from a childhood of trying to repair the lives around me, including my own. However, I have learned that being apologetic keeps a person humble. We should all apologize. It is a human way of exercising a very spiritual quality.

Day 65

I read this in the Victor Hugo novel Les Miserables:

> It is the same with wretchedness as with everything else. It ends by becoming bearable. It finally assumes a form and adjusts itself. One vegetates, that is to say, one develops in a certain meager fashion, which is, however, sufficient for life.

I believe the words poverty, hatred, discontentment, addiction, or even ignorance could be substituted for wretchedness. Poverty seems to be an all-encompassing word, however, and so I will focus on it. Poverty is not easily defined if you base it entirely on the concept of money. I think poverty can mean a wretched house where drugs and alcohol are prevalent or a home in which parents are not leading by example, or a home that truly is poor and the most fundamental aspects of life, such as food and clothing, become scarce. No matter what definition you give, poverty is something real among the children in our school, and every day I see students walk these hallways who are truly barely hanging on, but that is how they live. They barely hang on. Their lives have become bearable. It is a status quo that is hard to change. In fact, changing their lives requires breaking a toxic cycle that began before they were born. We must convince them they can accomplish goals, but this begins by teaching them they must set goals, a task for teachers that is sometimes littered with frustration. If you see a child or know a child you are sure is bound by some form of wretchedness, then you have an educationally moral obligation. You must intervene. How? Of course, only through thoughtful prayer and empathy will you find a way, but find a way you must.

Day 66

I know a man who does not love who he is. It has been a lifelong dilemma. He had to overcome a pathetic existence in childhood, filled with alcoholism and ignorance, dogmatic religious oppression, and ultimately his own weaknesses. He hated school. In fact, he feels even now as if school and several faculty members played an insidious role in creating the fear that seemed to dominate his youth. He has long since let go of bitterness, and he has forgiven anyone he thought he was angry with. In fact, he thinks perhaps that he was to blame for everything by being inadequate. Strangely, his attitude seems very much victim-like — a person who tries to repair the problems of others and in humility tries to take the blame because it seems a good way to cope.

I have tried talking to this man, and there are times when he seems to hear me and change his mindset, but at some deep level, he still struggles with the wounds, and his attitude toward education is at times cynical. He related to me a single incident involving a teacher in which he was ridiculed in front of classmates. This, he said, was just one of many, but he pointed out that was all it took to convince him that education is not a safe harbor for children. I know this man's story personally, and it is so very true. Let us this day be mindful that we have the power to build a future or tear it down. Let us be mindful that our tasks are ordained, and we must carry the souls of children in our hands to make sure they are safe and pointed in the right direction.

Day 67

There is a passage in the Bible that I sometimes read that I find astounding. Christ said to demand nothing in return for what we give. He said that those who beg must be given to, and we are to ask for nothing in return. This passage in Luke chapter 7 amazes me because it really hits at the core of human weakness. Giving is hard enough, but to simply give to a beggar without question and condition makes me think of the man on the street corner with the sign that states he will work for food or that he is homeless. I have heard people state that if he had the strength to beg, then he can work. Christ, of course, did not have this thought process, but He was God incarnate and saw the world through pure eyes. It could be that the mystery of Christ is pure vision, which we do not have. What would a child look like if our vision was pure or Christ-like, and what would we say if they were begging for anything at all, such as attention, food, clothes, help with homework, or just a kind word? I read this passage in Luke yesterday, and I prayed that God would give me the strength to give and give, and do so without so much as a shred of desire for return.

Day 68

Christ was a fisher of men. I think sometimes we deprive that concept of the profound respect it deserves. We see the symbol on a car bumper or hear the words spoken by a pastor, and then it fades away with our vanity as a society. Upon breaking down the concept, we should see that it means He was trying to save people. He was trying to intervene in their lives and literally rescue them. He walked all over the countryside, seeking out people who were willing to hear His words, and then He offered them a way to exist eternally. Now let us place this concept in the context of education. What if our goal was to fish for students? What if our sole purpose was to intervene and save them eternally? I think we might see them all differently. I think they might appear in need, and that would require that we take the approach of imperative intentions as if the end result were capable of grave consequences, and in reality, the consequences are indeed grave if we fail, just as Christ may have thought when mankind did not listen.

Day 69

When thinking of curriculum, I am confronted with the simple question of what to teach. Much of curriculum is simply based on what the educational hierarchy believes to be necessary to function from an economic standpoint or for college or university preparedness. From a purely secular viewpoint, I realize this is necessary. The newer mindset seems to be begging educators to teach critical thinking skills. This is not an easy task when our culture is so embedded in traditional methods that are both outdated and ineffective. Perhaps we should teach children to learn the eternally powerful skill of believing. Teach them the power of faith, in God of course, but also in themselves.

If you think about it, this requires human beings to develop deeply critical thinking skills. After all, a person of faith believes in the unseen, but to do so, it demands we search for God in our world and in our lives. People who have no faith in anything simply stop short of looking for answers and are content with whatever comes their way and whatever the outcome could be. People who believe possess an inner strength that also gives them vision that is unparalleled by ordinary sight. Faith is a powerful trait. I am certain it leads to higher-order thinking and certainly higher-order hope. From there we are able to search and explore our universe because we know ultimately, where it leads us. It is not blind faith that leads me to God, but instead, it is clear vision that allows me to search for God, and it is what I learn about my world that reinforces my faith.

Day 70

Are we correct to teach children evolution? I think it is necessary to teach evolution as a theory by a very intelligent man. The observations of Charles Darwin were amazing and quite logical to some degree. However, I cannot find a single scientific writing that gives me the ultimate answers to questions of creation. And I cannot seem to reach an agreement with Mr. Darwin about all of his intensely debatable writings. My own observations make clear to me that organic life does change through long-term adaptations, and some of those changes can be profound. Upon further observation, I have come to the conclusion that life began not by accident but by some divine spark. It is physically impossible for me to buy into the ideology that one mass of organic potential accounts for every living thing unless a being of such higher intellect that we cannot begin to fathom used that organic mass as a recipe to form all life. In other words, there are no answers for the deepest questions, and the search has exceeded even the explanations of Mr. Darwin. It makes believing in God all the more easier. The theory of evolution and natural selection is vital as we understand life, but it is merely a component of a larger picture painted by God.

Day 71

When I first began teaching the social sciences, I liked to focus on the events that led to the American Civil War. I have always been fascinated with our propensity to judge people based on race, and regardless of what theories are thrown about, I am personally convinced that our Civil War was fought over the issue of slavery. In fact, I have stated to students many times throughout my career that Abraham Lincoln was the greatest American president because he set free, through his decisions and courage, an entire race of people, and he did so in spite of half of our nation being willing to die as an adversary to his principles. Racism is a toxic and pathetic affliction. I have also stated to students that to be racist means you are small-minded and without a soul. You might think my assertions too harsh, but if you look acutely at racism, you begin to see that it is the product of evil, and it preys on ignorant people. We are obligated to teach diversity and be culturally responsible educators. The health of our planet depends on godly intentions.

Day 72

When I was a child, I was surrounded by men who I now term as scoundrels and unscrupulous thugs. They were poor role models on their best days, and I can only fall at the feet of God and Christ in the deepest gratitude that I broke free from their dark ways. Those men were gamblers, thieves, abusers of women, liars, and cheats and had no fear of God, which means scripturally they lacked wisdom, but I did not need anyone to point that out since it was painfully obvious.

But there was at least one glaring example of their weakness that I now realize may have been the most critical aspect of their lives that kept them from ever becoming decent men. They shunned any form of education. In fact, they never made an effort to better themselves whatsoever. They were like a pack of dogs running wild, with no boundaries, fighting over each morsel of food thrown out, and simply went from here to there with no goals of any type. They did not read books or watch movies. They did not have standards of conduct, only traits of survival. They were as ignorant as small children, except they were filled with bad intentions.

I wish I could paint a better picture, but the truth is colored by their actions, words, and legacies. Now as I look back I am convinced that had they realized the impact of a formal education, they would have lived different lives as younger men when their wives and children were trying to just get by day to day. I have through the years tried to describe my childhood, and I come up with only one word. It was a holocaust. Yes, I lived through it, but even that feels like a miracle when I think of the devilish incidents that made me question my own existence. Where this leads me to this day is the incredible need to convince children that an education could keep them from falling away from God. The less we know, the greater the likelihood that we will fall victim to temptations that might consume our lives. Poverty and ignorance are the work of evil. They combine to waste human lives.

Day 73

I thought last night as I lay in bed listening to the rain that our lives are meant to be lived in service. Christ served — a simple statement but so monumental. Today I challenge every person to serve someone else. I challenge myself to live my life for others and not for myself. There can be no greater compliment to Christ, and there can be no greater task for us. If every man or woman awoke tomorrow with the singular intention of giving all he or she has to others, our world would be utterly transformed in an instant. Wars would cease, hatred would crumble and die, lives would be saved, souls would be blessed, and God would be honored. There should be a class offered in our school on this imperative choice we should all make.

Day 74

It is the long winter. The snow hangs on until far into March and childhood moves slowly.

In the evening after supper, as the sun moves achingly into a cold void, we are put to bed.

The smell of her cooking drifts about the house and she turns down the heat for the night.

When the lights go out it takes a few minutes for my eyes to adjust and gradually the moon begins to shine.

Beams of light come through the window in slanted designs.

I arise from bed and open the window slightly, allowing the chill to glide into our room.

I curl under the blanket and realize that sleep will debate me for some time until I give in.

It is supposed to be spring, but of course winter is not in agreement and the landscape is frozen.

Snowflakes are sparse and they fall slowly against the glass.

Then I hear the sound coming from the oaks to the east of our house.

It is the owl, the barred owl, and it seems lonely, as if calling to a friend that it cannot find.

The call is repeated every few seconds and then it is silent.

Then it calls again, but it has flown closer to our house and it seems it is right outside my window in one of the big oaks near the yard.

I get up again and peer from the window trying to see it on a branch.

There it is!

It is a beautiful silhouette against the gray sky and just above the forest is the moon, Rising like a sign from God.

I would have given anything to be an owl for a few minutes or a few hours.

I would have flown across that lawn and into the forest.

All of the complicated issues of life are absent in the world of a child immersed in nature.

And like Emerson or Thoreau, I am philosophical, thinking perhaps that God is best explained by light and sounds.

I almost fall asleep looking at the shadowy figure of an owl and then it flies away. I do not want to go to school tomorrow.

I am comfortable here. I am safe here.

It seems like fiction, as if it happened in a book I read —
but I recall it happened.

Day 75

Special education, for the most part, offered to those students who do not possess disabilities in the extreme is a welfare state. It is an unrealistic method to educate children that have equally unrealistic outcomes. In the end, we in education simply hang a label on children that announces to the world they are different, slower, unequal, hindered, and ultimately less than normal, with no way of being great. When school has culminated, and these students graduate, they enter a world where there are not individualized education plans, no accommodations, no special education teachers — and this is not preparation by any stretch of the imagination.

I have always been an advocate of students being evaluated and met where they are by the teachers, and that teachers be hired based on their abilities to utilize varied instructional methods to reach whoever they are hired to reach and to do so with passion. Of course, in a perfect world there would be smaller classrooms and more one-to-one instruction, and in that perfect world there would be technology available to enhance the learning experience, but since the world is not perfect and we are limited in the purely secular sense, we must do it ourselves through divine intervention.

When our silly political system came up with the idea of "no child left behind," I laughed at such a concept, given the standards set forth by people who have never worked in education. If only every educator had thought long ago that no child can be left behind as opposed to waiting around for an elected person to discover what we should have all known when we got into this business! The Christian standard is straightforward. Everyone is equal, and a Savior who bled for us offers everyone the gift of life. I believe that education is imperative as well. The Scriptures are abounding with verses that stress the importance of studying the Bible. The modern literal translations, such as the English Standard Version, the New American Standard Bible, and the forthcoming Updated American Standard Version are written on a 10th and 11th-grade levels. How are we to follow the dozens of commands within Scripture that tells us to study God's Word, if we struggle to read or comprehend what we are studying? The good news of the kingdom is free, so too, let us take advantage of our free education as well. If we are left behind in school, might we not also be left behind in the deeper study of God's Word?

Day 76

I wonder if we realize how many of our students are living on the edge of hunger. I have noticed students in our school saving food and carrying it to the bus at the end of the day. I can easily ascertain the reasons why, and I do not think it is off base to suggest that too many of our children live without decent meals other than a school lunch or breakfast. It is amazing how much we take for granted in this society. We take for granted that every child is fed enough, and this is simply not the case. I have interviewed students who lived in shacks with broken windows or lived out of camper shells, and they thought the school food was their best meal of the day. We live in a country that builds churches that cost millions, where people worry endlessly about retirement pensions, carry credit cards to the max, drive vehicles that are exquisite, and pay high dollar for fuel and then gripe about it. Why can't we feed our own? What can be done to awaken the Christian soul of this society to the needs of our own? The real mission field is all around you.

Day 77

Today I had several encounters with administrators, and at least two of those encounters left me with a bad feeling. I think I walked away from the conversations feeling as if perhaps we as a team of leaders sometimes fail to humble ourselves. We live in a position of directing others, and through our flaws, we fail to make ourselves appear as equals or needing the help of others. I have been guilty of allowing my ego to get in the way before, and for that I am ashamed. The two men I spoke with today on the telephone simply made me collect my thoughts and conduct a self-inventory. Do I sound arrogant when I talk? Do I behave as if I know everything and do not need the advice and help of others? Am I approachable? God help me be humble if I fail to recognize these weaknesses. I have always thought of myself a leader, and in my heart, I care so much about people and what they feel and think. I pray today as the evening draws near that I love enough to get out of the way of God and others. I pray that I am of service to all. And I pray that my vision is clear regarding myself.

Day 78

Yesterday I thought of how I might appear to others, and I prayed that I was humble, a leader who could stay out of God's way. I prayed that my vision was clear regarding myself. Last night as I walked in our yard I thought of that self-inventory, and I came up with a rather unique perspective of myself. It seems that I am not intimidated by any person, yet I can be easily hurt by anyone. I suppose at the core of my soul is the simple desire to help others and to be a servant, and it is easy for a servant to suffer. Christ assured us that if we followed Him, there would be suffering. So it is today that I find myself pondering the immensity of that concept. I will suffer if I choose to be a Christian. Not an altogether wonderful ideology from a humanistic point of view, but through the Christ-centered point of view, it is a compliment and assurance we are on the right track. I think Paul said it best when he stated that he found contentment in all circumstances — and this man was in prison when he wrote those words. I wish to be happy. We all want to be happy. I think there has to be a way for us to find happiness in the midst of the trials because those trials will be there when we choose Christ.

Day 79

I had a child approach me today and ask if, since it was the Christmas season, he could have an a la carte item from the lunch menu, and he made this request with a smile. Since I know this child and have some knowledge of his home life, I find his request to be sad. I can imagine quite easily that he is hungry most days and we offer him a better world than his house. Just a few days ago, I entered my thoughts about hunger in this book of empathy, and this child only serves to illustrate the point with his simple yet penetrating words.

How could I say no? How could I look at that face and tell him that he should be just fine with lunch and that another item was not part of the plan? I have to admit I intend to help him out tomorrow because today I told him I could not. I have felt sickened all day regarding this. I think perhaps I will figure something out tomorrow and make sure he leaves with an extra item. I am always asking teachers to commit random acts of kindness, so I will do the same tomorrow and make sure it's chocolate. I have stashed some treats, and he seems the perfect subject to begin the day with. Just writing it makes me feel better.

Day 80

I was speaking to my son this morning regarding a book the two of us have read authored by Thomas Merton, and as I spoke of the deceased writer, I stated that he was a man who was part, Christ. I meant he was a man who possessed characteristics of Christ, such as humility, kindness, self-discipline, and perhaps a certain level of perfection in certain humanistic ways. I, of course, am not implying Thomas Merton was perfect, but as people go, he could have been closer than most. Christ actually expects us to try to attain perfection, this being scriptural. We as mortals tend to proclaim we are imperfect as if that will alleviate us of all expectations, but it is the effort to attain spiritual excellence that moves us closer to God. And the effort must be perfect, even if we are not.

Day 81

Let us ponder for a moment the immensity of pain that is caused by a parent who is unable to find any self-worth. The pain I am referring to is that which is experienced by the children of parents who feel little or no self-worth. It rubs off or filters down to the children. I know this to be true through experience and observation.

My own life is a testament to the reality of this pain. My parents — namely, my mother — had the best intentions, and it would prove to be their inability to break the cycle of our existence that led them away from their own education or any desire to improve themselves from a purely individual point of view. I have long felt pain for my mother, who had a brilliant mind, but no opportunity or support came her way because, during that age, it was a man's world, and the women I knew and loved were kept in fear and ignorance. And for my father, who simply chose the paths of least resistance and inevitably found his reality in booze, there was nothing but a paycheck-to-paycheck life that would not be conducive to contentment. Today we should look hard at the vast number of children in our school who are suffering from the pains of their parents, those who are filtering down emotions and bitterness that lend fuel to a cycle that is hard to break.

Day 82

I gave that boy some chocolate today. I also had a child pass by me at the crosswalk who boasted of his new shoes, purchased by his grandmother. There was another boy who passed by me in the cafeteria, and I noticed his shoes were literally falling apart. I asked him what size shoe he wore, and he was reluctant to tell me, but eventually did. I noticed another child in tears at a cafeteria table. He was sitting alone, and when I asked what had upset him, he too was reluctant to talk. I learned, however, that his lunch account was zero, and he was not eating today. I insisted on buying his lunch, and he was insistent that I not buy it. He eventually allowed me to help him.

I was reminded of a passage in a book I read long ago that spoke of a helpless and debilitated child who was begging along a roadside in the Himalayan Mountains. Her legs were deformed, and the author was entranced by her innocent and lovely smile. He wanted to help but somehow felt that in doing so, he would be taking her dignity. I have learned that my best intentions can sometimes cause as much pain as my worst intentions. May God give me the subtle and beautiful power of humility and the ability to leave another person's dignity untouched.

Day 83

What do you live for? We all live for something or someone, and some live for themselves. The deepest satisfaction and sense of self-worth comes from living for someone else. So long ago, a student athlete I was teaching and coaching at the college level came to me and wanted to talk about marriage. He was thinking about asking his girlfriend to marry him, but he was not sure. He asked me how he could know if he was ready for this big decision in life.

I thought about it for a moment and answered, "Let's say you were on your way to dinner with her tonight, and you were involved in an accident and she was injured. Her injuries caused paralysis from the neck down for the remainder of her life, and she was unable to bear children or have sex. You were forced to carry her to bed, help her with the most fundamental aspects of personal hygiene, and she even needed to be fed. Would you still love her and want to spend the rest of your life with her?"

He paused and thought about it, and after a few seconds of silence, I told him he was not ready. I said to him that love and sacrifice mean you look past what you want from life or what you deem to be happiness, and you assure God that you are not only willing but also spiritually ready to take on the pains and needs of another person and without hesitation. Love does not know limitations, and if a person could take on any task to lift up another, then most assuredly that is how we know God is in us. Living for someone else is the closest we will ever be to God in this world.

Day 84

My daily journal is about empathy. When all is said and done, I am reminded that to care so deeply for another that I feel that person's delights and sorrows is what life is all about. So it is that I am about to leave for Christmas break and see family, open gifts, eat myself full, and just feel good about those close to me. This month of December causes me to recall my youth and the holiday. In spite of the difficulties of childhood, it seemed that December was the one month when time stood still and hope was more than a falling star. I wrote this poem many years ago. It best explains my feelings, and it is my hope that all of you feel the same. I wish you a Merry Christmas.

December

Looking back across time's span
The gathering of our clan
At an old house for holiday
The night before Christmas day
As dark blanketed the homestead
The house smelled of cornbread
Of meat roasting while snow was falling
And the sounds of Mother calling
Kids at play in the landscape white
Ah, we could have played all night
But the meal the women did prepare
Was enchantingly waiting there
In the old house on the hill
Shivering in December chill
And yes, I can remember
The peace of December

Day 85

On this first day of the second semester, I am thinking of a favorite teacher from my past. I cannot produce a name. Schools have changed so much since my childhood. Instruction 40 years ago simply does not resemble modern practices. With that in mind, I cannot recall a class I enjoyed any more than another or a teacher who stood out as well. At some deeper level, this is not a heartwarming concept. I really should be able to remember a good influence, or perhaps the truth is there before my eyes and the reality is not a pretty picture after all. I recall names and faces but in a negative context only.

My formal education was limited to textbooks, discipline, popularity contests, drama, politics, and the hope it would snow every day and render the roads impassable so school would be canceled. I have, in fact, learned through reading, and down through the years, my appetite for books has grown. I realize now that literacy is the most profound tool available to teachers, and if a teacher could motivate a student to read and explore, then really when all is said and done, a student becomes a richer person in the long run. If you think about it, God could have left behind so much in the way of artifacts and monuments to embed His Word in our minds, but instead He left a Book.

Day 86

I am fascinated by Paul, the Apostle, the man once known as Saul of Tarsus. In biblical Scripture, his life is an obvious testament of how a man can go from being dreadful to saintly through the merciful love of God. Paul was really no better than any other genocidal villain in history. What I mean is that Paul persecuted and advocated the destruction of people based purely on their religious beliefs, and I refer to Christians, of course. I think the reason I am fascinated by Paul is because he admits to having been despicable and then transformed through the love of Christ. Moreover, he accepts the fact that he was once a criminal, and even in the grip of prison bondage, he proclaims his triumph of darkness and his love for God and Christ.

If we look closely at his personality, it is easy to see that he was a powerful man in his time and capable of great things; but in the end, he was humble and submissive to God. He is one of those characters in history I wish I could speak to and ask questions of. Reading his words has helped me to realize humility must be at the core of literally every word and thought in my being. I must be able to look back at all of my poor choices and mistakes as a man in need of God's mercy, and no matter how much future events may tax my soul, I must be content in knowing I am a better man because God rescued me from who I was.

Day 87

When all is said and done, what is a letter grade? Does an A or B or even an F really mean anything to a child other than points earned or not earned or points awarded for projects or tests? What if a child has an A but cannot master the materials or subject matter? What I am thinking is that grades are quite arbitrary unless the end result is mastery of something, and that means a teacher becomes the responsible party in determining if a student really gets it or not. Yes, I know we have to test, and yes, we have to document production or lack thereof, but that could be done in so many ways. The ultimate goal should be mastery, and that can take on different forms for different students.

I am reminded of the cartoon of various animals sitting in front of a teacher, and the teacher demands they all climb the tree. The elephant and the donkey look miserable because of course, they have no chance of succeeding. This leads me to the plain facts of the matter. All people are different, and it requires that we teach according to the person. This is not compatible with traditional methods or mindsets, and it asks us as educators to think outside the box. Now I will link this to the teachings of Christ. If you think about how He reached so many different people, you may come to the conclusion that He appealed to everyone. I think perhaps it may have been because He met people where they were and lifted them up. It is a simple concept really, but profoundly true. Teachers should bear this in mind.

Day 88

I am reminded today of a passage I read by the great author Norman Maclean in his short novel A River Runs through It.

> Eventually, all things merge into one, and a river runs through it. The river was cut by the world's great flood and runs over rocks from the basement of time. On some of the rocks are timeless raindrops. Under the rocks are the words, and some of the words are theirs. I am haunted by waters.[7]

I too am haunted by waters. I am reminded of the creek of my youth where I literally learned more science and mathematics than any classroom would ever teach me or any teacher would ever convey. It was there I felt safe. It was there I imagined a better world. I ran to that place and still do in my dreams. I can hear the murmur of the water and the sounds of birds and the wind. I can still see the giant sycamore trees with flaky white bark. Like old men, they stood there grinning at my childhood. It was my classroom because school was nothing more than an obligation at that time. Today, I ask all of us to venture to another place and take our students with us, teach them to dream and imagine and offer them a better education than possible in their own hinterland. We can begin by totally embracing the power of reading and turn them loose to find a destination that speaks to their souls.

---

[7] Norman Maclean, A River Runs Through It (Chicago, IL: University of Chicago, Press, 2001).

Day 89

Last night a friend sent me a message to let me know he is excited about our challenge. Last year, he and I decided to take on something that seems epic. We are both runners and trekkers, and here in our midlife it seems we need something to open the door to our souls. The epic challenge is a trek/run of a large section of the Ozarks Highlands Trail in Arkansas. This adventure will encompass about 32 miles, and our goal is to get close to or eclipse our record of 6 hours.

Last night as I fell asleep, there came over me a sense of peace that I had a purpose. I realize that not everyone thinks alike, and what is a challenge or purpose for me probably will not be so for another person. I slept soundly, with images of that trail moving in and out of my dreams. So it is today that I pray all people can find purpose. Our students each have such individual needs and desires, and we as educators owe it to them to be cognitive of those precious thoughts they possess. It is in their dreams that they search for who they are, and it is in reality that they sometimes get lost. I pray for my own strength to complete that trail, but there is no dread in my soul. Such is the case when we feel the calm of God in our dreams. It is there if you search it out. Bear in mind today that all people need a challenge, and they must set their own, but when people are lost and cannot find a goal, then it is up to you as a teacher to reach inside of their souls and expose the dream to them. What a wonderful gift we can give children when we show them a mountain summit and then provide them with the tools and confidence to climb it.

Day 90

Many years ago, I served as an Arkansas State Trooper for a short term. Of course, I have many memories, but there is a person who served to create the most vivid and impressionable recollections. He was the drill sergeant who trained me and spent three months serving as a mentor and teacher to me. He was an amazing man, imposing, and intent upon finding limits in each of us and then pushing further until perhaps we broke or improved. He was the consummate teacher and gentleman beneath an exterior that was intimidating. But now, so many years later as I reflect, he was without a doubt the man in my life I measure myself by — the man I look upon as the male role model who made me who I am today. His strict regimens and discipline, the rigid voice and firm demeanor, all forced me to look within, and ultimately, I grew up, improved, and really became a clear minded man. I miss him sorely, and there have been times when I literally was in tears thinking of him and the impact he had on my life. If each of us could have this impact on just one other person, I think the world might improve exponentially.

Day 91

The assistant principal in my building impressed me so much on a day not long ago by becoming emotional over the plight of one of our students. I know the tears were sincere. It has happened more than once. I wonder if she realizes I notice the subtle pains she sometimes feels for kids. She has a heart that is ripped open with compassion when she sees a child in need. I watched as her eyes slowly welled up, and it left me with the greatest sense of peace that I work alongside a person who truly gets it and wants our children not only educated but also to have a richer, fuller life, and it is evident in her demeanor. Some administrators forget to be teachers. She has not forgotten our mission. She is capable of being in my role, in any role, and I am humbled by her commitment.

Day 92

We are still children. Never forget this. In ways that sometimes evade our adult eyes, we are still in our youth. I wrote this about myself many years ago:

> I still talk to myself, repeat my words as if I am calmly schizophrenic, but it is a practice that began when I was a child and it has stayed with me much like my habit of playing with my ear when I am nervous or unable to release the pent-up energy within.

Look closely at who you are, and see if the child is visible. If you are able to find the child within yourself, then look at our children in this school with the new vision that perhaps left you long ago. Teaching sometimes requires that we think like children. I would submit to you that teaching sometimes demands that we be children.

Day 93

I have developed a fascination with the poetry of William Butler Yeats. I think because I learned of my Scottish/Irish lineage, I wished to know more of my past and the people who helped form me, even those I never could have known. He wrote one poem that I find myself reading time and again. I feel confident I read it repeatedly because at some deep level I feel it speaks for me. It is titled, "The Stolen Child." Here is a brief excerpt:

> For he comes, the human child, To the waters and the wild
> With a faery, hand in hand,
> For the world's more full of weeping
> Than he can understand.

I think our world is too filled with weeping, and certainly more than children can understand. I write so much about childish pains and sorrows. I suppose it is because I wish for people to understand what happens to children because of adult blunders and bad intentions. As an educator, it is paramount that I focus on children and not data, curriculum, or even grades. It is the person that matters the most.

The poem is a story really. It is about the imaginary world of the mythological faery coming to take a child away from the sorrows of life and on to a safer place filled with unlimited potential. In fact, I have read an analogy that Yeats was writing of heaven. Yeats focuses on the power of nature throughout the lines of this timeless poem. Think about it. The waters and the wilds are where the faery takes the child. It is that place, according to Yeats, away from tears. So much can be said by a poet. I remind us all in education that children will hide if they are hurt or do not understand our actions and words. In our school, there should be no weeping, and each classroom should be that place of waters and the wild.

Day 94

Through education, I have determined that children are a product of their own imaginations, not just environment or genetics. Children learn differently and have markedly different needs. It is with great hope that I begin every day on a mission to enlighten adults to the psychology of teaching because, you see, it is very much a psychological endeavor. One must see deep into the human mind, all the way to the soul, to determine how a child can be successful. And so I ask you if you are able to see another person's soul. It is not a simple endeavor. It requires that you possess empathy and humility. There is no way to see the spirit of another human being unless you have developed your own sense of awareness about yourself. In other words, you must feel your own mistakes before seeing another person's faults. You must feel sorrow before you can see it. You must feel pain before you can experience it on behalf of another person. Teaching is not simply an exercise, but instead it is a revelation.

Day 95

Is love part of our curriculum? I ask this question because it is in my view the single most important aspect of the human condition. It protects us. It strengthens us. It saves our lives and souls. I wrote this excerpt as part of my book The Voice of Water. It is about my wife, and I wanted you to read and feel the words as my expression of how love can be taken so very seriously.

In the darkness of the room, I hear her breathing. She gently turns to me and drapes an arm over my chest. In the stone-like silence, I can literally feel the beating of her heart. The woman here with me is eternal, she must be. Otherwise, nothing makes sense, and I need sensibility like I find in nature, in order to see God clearly. I awake in the night from dreamy travel. I dream almost every night. She is still there. She has always been there. I think I loved her before I met her; certainly I wished for her all of my life. I still hear her breathing and in my groggy state of mind half in and half out of fatigue, I liken it to something. Perhaps it resembles a heartbeat or a rhythmic song, or the sound of her is like the distant echo of the soul as it calls out for love. I know that sound. It was a sound I learned long ago. A gentle hum as if some great force was rocking in a chair and easing music from within. It is the hum of perpetual motion, moving life, dynamic thought; the very essence of God. That hum of her breathing is the hum of the water as it moves through me, just as she does and I know love is like water that never ceases its journey.[8]

The reason I share this today is because I wanted us to look at the Word as if it were something life-sustaining, and teach our children it is not to be taken lightly. We should offer them the Word as part of who we are and what we hope for in every person. It somehow must be part of our daily lives, and it should be seen in everything we say and do. A person can only be close to God through love. To suggest otherwise is simply the words of disillusionment.

---

[8] Terry Jamieson, The Voice of Water (St. Louis, MO: PenUltimate Press, Inc., 2008).

Day 96

I think we have an obligation to teach children to be environmentalists. It is blatantly wrong to overlook the need to educate people about the fragility of the earth as we utilize it in seemingly endless ways. Mankind expects so much from the physical world, and we take so much for granted. We appear to expect the earth to heal and to provide. I am quite sure I have a deeper viewpoint than the average person on this issue. I see the earth as possessing some level of divinity and look upon nature in all forms as a being to be cherished. Poets long ago looked upon the world in ways that suggest mankind was living on a globe that was very much a physical and spiritual being. It is shameful that modern man, for the most part, looks upon the world as an endless supply for insatiable needs. Our students must be taught to possess a reverence for the earth, and perhaps the next generation will protect what this generation has raped. I am sure God would ask us to add it to our curriculum if we were to ask in prayer.

Day 97

A Thought for the Day

I wondered what I would say if I were running down a lonely dirt road and suddenly came upon Jesus Christ standing there looking at me as if He needed to know something. I paused and stood there with Him, knowing I owed Him an explanation for why I needed to clean my soul when it had already been washed by His death.

"So where do I stand in all of this?" He asked.

I have thought long about this answer.

"I love You, Lord, and I respect with the greatest deference Your willingness to die for me." And then I begged Him to understand that I worked for Him out of love, that I could not sit still and expect Him to pay it all, to do it all for me, and I feel worthless if I cannot have a little something to do with my cleansing. I need to pay some debt. Otherwise, I feel as if I have been a freeloader on the purest, meekest person who ever walked the planet. He smiled at me and shook His head. Laughter followed.

"Just so you know, I made sure your soul was clean when you asked Me to be your Savior," He said. "I don't mind you loving Me so much that you feel the need to show it by taking some of the load, but understand that I have saved you a ticket on the last train whether you do this or not."

Day 98

I am concerned about my mother this morning as she prepares for her surgery. I am reminded of her plight through my childhood: trying to raise two boys alone, sending us to school every day, hoping someone at school would care as much as she did, living in a man's world trying to be both parents, and all the while shedding tears because her worry was sometimes greater than the pains. Life is so short. We are nothing more than a flash of light in a dark night, but we can burn so very brightly. Our light can shine like the sun, even if it is only for a moment. I write these words as I prepare to go see her. I have always wanted her to be able to look back and know she was my greatest teacher. Her life was hard, and seeing her struggle brings me to tears. But God protects the meek, and she qualifies. Today she will win a battle. I am confident of this. And if I am wrong in the worldly sense, then most assuredly she taught me to fight and never give up. Today I asked my assistant principal to show the teachers a video of a man who climbed Mt. Kilimanjaro. He is a paraplegic. My mother pretty much raised me without the legs of another. I bear this in mind as I drive toward her this morning.

Day 99

I met the surgeon last night following Mom's triple bypass. He was a very kind man. He was from India, I think. He spoke for about ten minutes, carefully going over the surgery he performed. After a few minutes, I was struck by something. This man has talents and intellect that go beyond my understanding. He is capable of saving lives. In fact, he does it every day, and few people give it a thought after he leaves the room. But I did. I was suddenly feeling the deepest respect for his education and training, the deepest respect for his commitment, and as he paid us a smile and farewell, I turned to my wife and said, "I had no idea Superman was from India." As an educator, I should have an obligation to God to build people like that man, to train morally and through academics people who will make a difference. I do not need to concentrate on grades or curriculum but instead on the people. In the end, my goal has to be superheroes and not data.

Day 100

There is a passage in the Bible in which Paul writes of being con- tent in all things. When he wrote those words, he was in prison for his ministry. I have often analyzed the writings of Paul, and I am amazed by his level of enthusiasm in spite of his circumstances. In fact, it is hard to find another person in the pages of history who had a greater impact on mankind, and he did it in the worst of conditions, I presume. I mean, who in their right mind would want to be in prison unless at some deep level he looked at it as a cause?

I have been reading the works of Victor Frankl, an Austrian psychologist who spent time in a concentration camp during the Nazi regime, and he spoke of man needing meaning or a purpose to survive. I have gradually drawn some parallels between Paul and Frankl. They each were in a difficult circumstance yet found something that gave their lives meaning. Both were persecuted for their beliefs. Frankl was a Jew, and the Nazis were, of course, murdering the Jewish people. Paul was a Christian, converted from his previous life of having persecuted Christians. Both men looked upward. They each extended the hands of their spirits to a greater love. When we are mired in the daily routine, we should imagine we are in a place of difficulty for a purpose greater than our comfort. It places us in good company.

Day 101

Victor Frankl wrote in his book Man's Search for Meaning that there came a point during his bondage in a concentration camp — Auschwitz, to be specific — in which he became comforted by thoughts of his wife and the love they shared. Here is that excerpt.

> We stumbled on in the darkness, over big stones and through large puddles, along the one road leading from the camp. The accompanying guards kept shouting at us and driving us with the butts of their rifles. Anyone with very sore feet supported himself on his neighbor's arm. Hardly a word was spoken; the icy wind did not encourage talk. Hiding his mouth behind his upturned collar, the man marching next to me whispered suddenly: "If our wives could see us now! I do hope they are better off in their camps and don't know what is happening to us."

> That brought thoughts of my own wife to mind. And as we stumbled on for miles, slipping on icy spots, supporting each other time and again, dragging one another up and onward, nothing was said, but we both knew: each of us was thinking of his wife. Occasionally I looked at the sky, where the stars were fading and the pink light of the morning was beginning to spread behind a dark bank of clouds. But my mind clung to my wife's image, imagining it with an uncanny acuteness. I heard her answering me, saw her smile, her frank and encouraging look. Real or not, her look was then more luminous than the sun which was beginning to rise.[9]

We must be able to believe in another person, to have faith in that person. Without it, we are alone to face sometimes insurmountable obstacles. God wants us to love another person and believe in that person. Frankl wrote something I have always believed in. He spoke to me in the acutest manner when I read that passage. It hits at the core of what we need as human beings, and to suggest otherwise is simply naïve.

---

[9] Victor Frankl, Man's Search for Meaning;
http://www.goodreads.com/quotes/802681.

Day 102

I recall hearing the immortal words of Kermit the frog.

What's so amazing that keeps us stargazing? And what do we think we might see?

Someday we'll find it, the rainbow connection, The lovers, the dreamers, and me.

As this song plays in my mind, I wonder which of these I am, or perhaps I am both.

And what is wrong with being a dreamer?

What is life without dreams, and what are we if not children looking for a star in the sky that just might be our own?

Do you remember how this song goes?

Sing it to yourself, and admit it feels good.

Day 103

Why are some kids followers and some leaders? I wonder if we could really see a leader among our students. I think sometimes schools falsely believe leadership is defined by those students who are in clubs and organizations or make the best grades or perhaps are in the National Honor Society. I have learned otherwise. Leaders are those with integrity, the will and desire to help others, and moreover, the need to excel. Sometimes these traits are not so obvious.

I once sat in a meeting with other teachers trying to vote on students for National Honor Society. It ended up being a group of adults behaving like kids. After a while, I wished I had never agreed to help. Several of the finest students in our school were left out because they were not popular. Now I realize this may have been my viewpoint, but it was hard to feel otherwise. I am convinced two girls were left off the final list because the teachers in the room simply did not like them. The two girls were quiet and not outgoing, according to one of the teachers. The girls were not in any organizations. They were not athletes. They were outstanding students with exemplary records. They were filled with integrity. They were decent and kind to all who came in contact with them. In fact, they were Christians in every sense of the word. The two girls were heartbroken about not being selected. I vowed to never participate again, and I have not.

I learned that leadership is really innate, and the average person could not select a leader based on the criteria of worldly ideologies. Leaders should be those people who are filled with Christlike love and qualities. I wonder in our clouded modern judgment if we could pick out a future leader in a classroom filled with children. I am inclined to think most kids are followers, even those we are sure are not. They follow the world and try to impress us with their accomplishments while the quiet workers plot the course for us all.

Day 104

I was reading last night from the memoirs of Jane Goodall, and her words left me with thoughts of how it is that we so often do not understand the points of view of others. As a Christian, it is important to have clear vision, the ability to see the world in so many facets and colors. How can Christianity reach out to the masses, those people of other lands who do not understand the message of Christ or have never heard the words, unless we are open to comprehending their way of life, why they believe differently, or what cultural barriers need to be bridged? I offer to you that when and only when you are able to see another perspective different from your own will you be able to possess empathy, reach out to another person, and connect.

Day 105

I find myself looking at the night sky, wondering just how many mysteries we would find if we were able to fly to all those galaxies that exist so evident to the naked eye. Using simple binoculars, I am amazed at what I see: the Pleiades, the Orion Nebula, and Jupiter. As a child I would stare at the stars, imagining what it might have been like for ancient cultures to use the sky for navigation and why some of those cultures thought the very moral foundations of the universe was found in the heavens. I think the greatest marvel of the night sky is the sheer magnitude of the sky itself. The mathematics of space leaves no doubt in my mind that God exists. It is not that I need a reminder. It is just another way that I stay humble about my existence.

Day 106

To be a Christian means to understand those people you intend to inform of the love and salvation offered by Christ. This means we must comprehend all other cultures and religions at a very intricate level. It means we must know the peoples of our world, their ingrained beliefs, and customs, to better grasp what is needed to reach them. Putting this in simplistic terminology, to be a Christian is to know a Buddhist, a Hindu, a Muslim, a Jew, and the list goes on and on. We must know them to reach them. We cannot be intimidated by other cultures. We cannot be arrogant about other cultures. We cannot be blind to what people think, feel, and believe. Christ was open to loving everyone. It is our obligation to do the same, and perhaps the end result will be connectivity.

Day 107

Teaching children about sexuality should be a parental obligation. The reality is, of course, that most parents do not teach their children about life and those sensitive aspects that become issues later on. Schools do have the same obligation, but the curriculum is difficult to write. It could be that schools have to step out, risk criticism, and go forward with something that works. Society allows sexuality to be at the forefront of virtually every medium we know of, and because we are bombarded with skin and immorality, the end result is insensitivity toward what should have been a beautiful and sacred part of our lives. Education should look no further than Christian principles to find a curriculum that works. Placing it in proper context is a strong beginning, and from there we can demonstrate that sexuality is normal but must be kept within the boundaries of marriage. Parents would support sex education if it were morally constructed, with Christian intentions. The liberality of current think tanks only scares parents and prevents educators from offering an important learning experience to the masses.

Day 108

In these brief words today, I offer up the question: Can we teach love?

Can we even define the word? Is it a word that represents different views and emotions to different people? I doubt anyone could argue against the fact that a child not taught love is a lost child. It is a word that means life. It is the blood in the veins of the human soul. It is the reason people hate. I am convinced love can be pure or toxic, and those people who do not understand the word are easily duped into hating.

Day 109

I recently read a book about people who are skeptics and people who are believers. There was a passage that really touched me deeply. I have always been profoundly moved by creation, the natural world, magnificent events and outcomes, and throughout my life, I have felt that education opens our minds to God as much as any other venue. It is what we know about our world that I find amazing. The passage read:

> Miracles are explainable; it is the explanations that are miraculous.[10]

I realize that it is a matter of perspective. I believe in miracles. The world and all components are miraculous, and the fact that God created it only adds to the wonder. I like the idea that education discovers miraculous aspects of our universe because it is through knowledge that I see God clearly. Ignorance has no view of God. What a wonderful blend it is to look at education as a way to grow closer to God.

---

[10] Tim Robinson, Stones of Aran (New York: NYRB Classics, 2008).

Day 110

Love should empower. Love should not enable. As educators, we should empower children to be strong, make good decisions, stand up for all that is right, be unselfish, and moreover, tell the truth and live that truth. Far too many parents love in ways that end up weakening children. They wish for their children to never fight a battle or never shed a tear, and although it is hard to be a spectator, we help if our love creates strength. Sometimes that requires we get out of the way and allow experience to help them. That might also require that we get out of the way of God.

Day 111

Some people are in a deep ravine and have two choices: stay and die or trek out. I have observed countless people mired in circumstances or held bondage by some vice and be unable to escape because being at the bottom of that ravine is comfortable. In fact, such sayings as, "You have to die of something," or "This is just who I am," or "I can't change," are all words of self-defeat. I think educators should teach self-control and the willpower to overcome obstacles, because most assuredly all people will run into obstacles. Those with the power to overcome trek out and those without it simply languish in the ravine until even the view to the top is obscured by doubt and futility.

Day 112

Yesterday one of the finest teachers in this district stated that she had discovered empathy after all these years, and I immediately held even greater respect for her. She is truly one of the best in this district, with a track record to prove it, and she helped the teachers around her with her honesty and sincerity. Sometimes we can work so hard at this profession that the windows become clouded by the grime of life. The view is lost in our efforts and best intentions. Doing this every day becomes a powerful routine that drains us of our spiritual eyesight. I too have been in that place where my view was clouded, and then I wiped out my eyes and saw empathy. I have come to work every day this year respecting this great teacher. Now she appears even larger.

Day 113

I recall a school board meeting once upon a time in which a board member made a racist remark. I sat in disbelief while the other members chuckled. Even now as I look back on that moment, I am reminded that school board members must be held to the same high standard as all other members of the educational culture. This passage today may seem harsh, but if I am, to be honest, it must be communicated.

Most school board members have no idea what it means to be an educator. They are people who live and work outside of the realm of education and meet with school leadership about once a month to discuss pertinent matters in the district. Unless they choose to really get to know their school district, they will only rely on the school superintendent in most cases to learn about whom they serve. There is a multitude of great people serving schools in this role. There are a few that have agendas and hurt schools. I have seen both. Ultimately, they choose to be an advocate for all members of the district, or they can participate in what might bring a school down. I think that godly and educated community members are essential to holding a school accountable, and without those prerequisites, a district could be at the mercy of a person who damages a school in such a way that it takes years to repair the wounds. Let us be mindful today that our need for godly educators includes board members as well.

Day 114

I recall leaving a university parking lot nearly three decades ago, having taken a final exam to complete the requirements of a bachelor's degree in geography, and feeling that I had been set free from a cycle of jumping through hoops. There were some classes that piqued my interests but overall my experience was obvious in my very average grade point. I was unsure of where I was headed. I had lost any hopes of achieving childhood dreams, and with no direction or tutelage, I was destined to wonder and wander. I thought of heading west to the Rocky Mountains for a try at the wilderness guide profession. I thought of law enforcement, a profession I would have a brief stint with later on, but ultimately I arrived at coaching more than likely because I could not put away my dreams of an athletic career.

Not many years later, my coaching vocation landed me in the classroom as a teacher and suddenly I arrived at a palpable realization. I was a teacher. It came naturally to me. I liked the philosophy of teaching, the essence of revelation, finding answers, and elevating people to reach their dreams. As I reflected on the years of youth and the dreams I could not realize, it became obvious to me that I wanted others to find their dreams. Gradually I came to know myself as a teacher, and given my lackluster academic performances in a public school and through those early university years, it was odd that I should be in such an important academic role.

Recently I was reflecting on what I have learned as a teacher and educational administrator. If I were to be asked what the most vital aspect of education is, my answer would no doubt discourage the pundits of the field. In all my years, I have observed that data stays constant. Graduation rates, attendance rates, and test scores have basically been consistent, at least in the districts I have been associated with. Sure there are some fluctuations, but in the grand scheme there has been little change. There has been a multitude of professional development visions and obscene amounts of money spent on programs to enhance learning, and it seems the numbers stay the same. I think it is because educational leadership in all of its arrogance has failed to grasp some simple mindsets.

It is not the pedagogy. It is the people.
It is not the data. It is the demographic.
It is not the curriculum. It is the culture.

In the years since my formal education I realize that much if not all of what I have learned has come from my own research and reading. I suppose the one aspect of my education that I can thank someone for is the fact that I can read. Teaching me to read helped me overcome my weaknesses and those of the educational process as a whole. This is harsh but it is so very true and it does not have to be this way. Schools cannot be diploma mills intent on gathering taxpayer money to pay for the ambitions of misguided political egos. Schools must be havens for young people to dream and explore, to be whom they wish to be, and in the end to participate in a harmonious world that demands higher level thinking.

Day 115

This past Wednesday evening, I lectured a college class on the topic of construal level theory. I have become a student of human perspective. It is becoming increasingly obvious to me that one of the most glaring reasons why people fail is because they cannot see past the moment. Psychologists view this in terms of construal theory. If you can, try to visualize a long-range goal, and then ask yourself why you are confident you can reach that goal. Most people who can see the light at the end of the tunnel are looking for it. Those who cannot see the light merely exist, and they are likely to fail or struggle immeasurably. I feel confident that teachers can be susceptible to this through the years because the routine can drag them down until their vision becomes less and less. Set goals. It's really that simple and cannot be overemphasized. In addition, we should demand children learn this precious life skill. Scripture even states that our lives should be focused on the goal of eternity.

Day 116

You can sit in a pew or sing hymns. You can read Scripture daily and study it until you know every passage. You can believe with the faith of a child. You can tell others about Christ and spread the Word. But you are not a Christian until you live it. And really teaching is the same. You can know it all, but it is not until you feel it, become an example of it, live it, and express it that you become a teacher. The only way a person can find this enlightened place in life is through empathy. The mind that loves is the mind that is close to God.

Day 117

Galileo said, "I do not feel obliged to believe that the same God who has endowed us with sense, reason, and intellect has intended us to forgo their use."[11]

This is a lesson to all Christians. We cannot simply dismiss our obligation to search for knowledge or truths because we are afraid of what we will find. Instead, our God has bestowed the ability upon us to grow intellectually, and we have a moral obligation to teach children that knowledge is attained through those gifts from God.

---

[11] Galileo Galilei, http://www.brainyquote.com/quotes/quotes/g/galileogal161381. html.

Day 118

The ability to show love or express love and the desire to do so are traits of a true Christian. A person able to act on feeling is a person in touch with God. Christ was active. He was traveling by foot to as many places as he could visit, and he was constantly demonstrating love to people. I ponder this aspect today because I know people who simply are unable to express feelings or show what is in their hearts, and it leaves me with the emptiness they provide. Life is too short for us to deny others the beauty of our hearts filled with caring. It only takes a moment today for you to edify another person, shake a hand, hug a friend in need, fill your spouse with eternal kindness, encourage your son or daughter, and failing to do so is really narcissistic if you are truthful to yourself. It amazes me how the routines of life begin to erode the human spirit, and people grow distant from one another, and it happens to Christians when it should not. In fact, Christians owe it to their Savior to never allow this to happen. You cannot worship God on Sundays, read the Bible, and pray, and then spend the remaining time of your week denying those around you of commitment.

Day 119

I think educators should sign a contract with schools, parents, and children. Last night as I lectured my college class, I spoke of how it seems our young people all follow broken role models, musicians who sing foul lyrics, actors, and actresses who advocate immoral causes, sports stars who behave like thugs, and reality television that is most certainly unreal. Educators cannot become like those poor models. We must polish ourselves, maintain the posture of Christ, and moreover, agree we will always be that light on the hill to children and parents. I will go so far as to suggest that any person in education who is unable to live up to these expectations must consider another profession. We owe it to the advancement of decency. We owe it to our children and their parents. We owe it to God.

Day 120

I found no relevance in school. I educated myself. This is a reality. Now that I am a middle-aged man, I can assess the roots of my education, the progression, and ultimately the maturity of my being, and the vast majority of what I have learned came from the pages of books. This is not to suggest I was without the influence of teachers. I am, however, stating that much of what I built upon was found in the readings that have enriched my life. Books are powerful, even more, powerful than a classroom, especially in the hands of an eager reader. I cannot recall a foundation for mathematics other than very basic principles. I taught myself algebra because it was not required that I take the class in high school. There were no expectations other than rudimentary skills. Of course, I realize, now that I am an educator, that people responsible for teaching me all those years ago were only carrying out what was expected in that era, and moreover, the entire system was sort of Stone Age compared to now. I have long since decided that if I am to be a teacher, then I will expect great things from people, and I will be a lifelong student. In addition, I will offer the beauty of books and the written word as if their lives depend upon it. Mine certainly did.

Day 121

Can you put a face on God? Can you describe God? Be careful that your answer does not smack of legalism. Is your God:

- a God of words you read in Scripture,
- a God of prayer when you are alone,
- a God you cannot see,
- a God you cannot feel,
- a God you confess sins to,
- a God you cannot be angry with,
- a God that destroys nonbelievers,
- a God you are afraid of,
- a God that cannot be shared,
- a God of men only, or
- a God that wants you to believe forsaking knowledge?

I ask this because my God may be different from your God.

My God is the God of complex life and processes.

My God is the God of love and empathy for any person who is searching for hope.

My God is not a man or a woman but a Spirit, who is not partial to man or woman, nor bigoted.

My God is a provider of miracles, and I know this because creation is filled with miracles.

My God is closer to me when I am in love with a mortal.

My God is not imaginary.

My God's qualities are clearly seen from the world's creation, such as the sunrise, the green of life, the sound of music, and when I feel the heartbeat of another.

My God is the teacher of sacrifice.

Day 122

Before you assume all people can overcome their circumstances, it might help if you could see the circumstances. Perhaps judgment would be less likely if you knew:

- that a child is hungry every day because at home, there is little more than rice and bread,

- that a child is living with a mother and father who are uneducated and bitter, both unable to move away from poverty,

- that a child is watching a father abuse a mother,

- that a child is watching a parent abuse drugs, taking pills and languishing in the grip of meth,

- that a child is surrounded by racism,

- that a child is held tightly by religious legalism,

- that a child is suffering from health issues because parents cannot afford even rudimentary treatments,

- that a child has nothing to read in a home that has ever promoted any aspect of education,

- that a child is told daily that he or she will never amount to anything, and

- that a child needs school!

Yes, needs school!

Because it is the safest place, he or she will know in a 24-hour time span.

I see children every day who struggle because where and what they come from is so powerful that reading, writing, and any other aspect of our curriculum seem trivial next to their plight of survival. Think twice before you judge.

Day 123

A woman came into my office to ask that her child be withdrawn from school so she and her live-in boyfriend could commence homeschooling her son. I attempted to talk her out of it, but it was clear she was passionately intent on going through with her plan. Then she astounded me with her reasoning as to why. She looked directly at me as my assistant sat and observed the exchange and told me she knew I was leading a conspiracy to brainwash our students and I was working for the government. The look on my face was most surely one of incredulity, or maybe I appeared stupefied. I could think of only one thing to say in response to her statement. I told her I was sorry for her that she actually believed such a thing and simply shook my head in painful sorrow. Make no mistake — there are people who are lost in our society raising children to be lost.

Day 124

I have in previous writings touched on the need for us to be apologetic to one another. Here is the view from a child.

The Apology (A child's view from the pew)

Now as I look back, it would have seemed a very simple remedy for most spiritual ailments. As I grew older, I came to realize people just could not say they were sorry. You know a child can learn so much sitting or walking alone in a forest or wading in a creek. Church just did not possess the same power to me.

The preacher would gradually raise his voice until he was shouting, and he managed to explain in an hour all the ways we could get to hell. Laced in his words like subliminal messaging was the dire importance of repenting of sins. I heard him. I heard every word I could stand to hear because after a while, a little guy just could not hold on to reality. Then as I fell away from the sound of his voice, I would find myself in those natural places that harbored far more peace, serenity, and answers to critical questions. In other words, I suffered from attention deficit disorder and still do. A colleague recently called it a sugar high, not realizing I was offended by his remark, but the preacher did not understand me either. The more I think about it, teachers didn't as well, which might explain why I taught myself math and science. I seemed to be the only teacher capable of having patience for me.

Now back to that apology people can't seem to conjure. I think I have a theory about why. Repenting of sins to God is easy. Folks just go to a quiet place and tell God they are sorry. Being that God rules the universe, it would seem a safe gesture on our part. No one can hear except God, and no one can judge except God, so we just roll out the apologies until we think all is clean again. Now, that having been established, I think you can see where I'm going. People just can't humble themselves to one another like they do with God. I don't know if it's because we are afraid we might appear weak or wrong, but either way, we avoid doing the most vital act of the soul and that's feel empathy.

Looking back and recalling that tiny country church, I almost hear the shouting and the demands we repent. I can almost raise my hand like I'm in class and blurt out my childish questions. "How come ya'll don't say you are sorry to each other and then make things right? How come ya'll are only able to repent to the Lord?"

Of course, had I blurted out those questions, I would have met with some punitive measure, so it was safer to just pretend I was climbing Everest or fishing for trout, or diving in the ocean, or hiking a trail, or collecting crayfish, and I suppose nature and I just had an agreement that when I could not solve the problems of life I could just go outside and find the answers.

Day 125

I have a photograph of my brother carrying a wolf over his shoulders. He studied wolves in northern Minnesota when he was a young man. The image is ingrained in my memory because it was a time when he was truly content and looked at life as a spectacular journey. He loved being in that vast wilderness. He is and always has been a zoologist. I knew he would be when we were just children. Sometimes when I look at that image, I am reminded of how he and I imagined we were animals. It is strange how as children we can dream or aspire to greater heights through our imaginations, and sometimes our imaginations seem farfetched. But make no mistake through casual observations of children. They dream and aspire to enormous things, and it is for some a way to survive life. So many children are subjected to failure and hopelessness at home. If you can cultivate the dreams of children, then you can save their lives. That photograph of my brother is in my office. My brother is a teacher, and I consider him the finest professor of biology I have ever observed. The reason I think he is gifted as a teacher is because of his innate love of the science of his discipline. Can you say that about yourself? Are you a student of your subject matter? Are you a child of your dreams? Even now in my middle age, I am a dreamer. I always will be.

Day 126

Do not think teachers are only found in schools. Many years ago when I first came here and took on the position of head soccer coach, I was faced with a dilemma. The program was new, and there was no youth program in large scale, certainly not the type of program to develop players in numbers. There were a few dedicated parents. The issue for me was how to create a developmental program outside of school for children in lower grades. I began to research people locally to determine who might be a good candidate to lead a youth developmental program, and several key traits were required. I needed a man or woman with patience, the ability to keep kids enthused, an open mind to learn the game, and the temperament to handle children in all of their positive and negative states of mind. I met a man, a kind man, and instantly I was certain he could handle it. He agreed to do what I wanted to develop the kids for the future of the high school program. Many years later, after a multitude of players came through the youth soccer school we had created, we reaped the rewards of winning. Many of those kids went on to play in college. That man is directly responsible for so much of their success and my own. Teachers are not made; they are natural. It is such an intrinsic skill, and no classes in any university can prepare a person for it, as I have stated so many times. I see him almost weekly. He works in a local cafe, and I think it is fair to say he has many friends. Each time I see him, I am reminded that he was a teacher.

Day 127

I am thoughtful this morning of the culture of our region. I grew up in the Ozarks, and I have always understood the people. It is a place sometimes removed from the rest of the nation. I know this because I recall certain aspects of my youth that smacked of isolation. I heard a relative say that when I left home to go to college, I would have my first encounters with black folks. I was told it was safe in the hills, where we were surrounded by family and people we knew, and that when I went to college, I would be exposed to a world saturated in sin and misfortune.

I learned, however, a bleak truth. The hills I grew up in were hidden away from reality and moreover hidden from a better life and a better understanding of others. Bigotry and racism were obvious traits of the world I grew up in, and it was not until I became educated to cultures outside my own that I realized just how restricted I had lived. I did not eat in a fancy restaurant until I was in college. I did not travel more than two hours from home until I was an athlete in college and saw the American South as a whole. It was through traveling that I became aware of the isolation of ignorance and the ignorance of isolation. I grew to understand the imperativeness of knowing other cultures. I suppose the ultimate revelation was that parents sometimes hold children back because they are held back by their own limitations, and those limitations are most assuredly avoidable.

I am reminded of the motion picture The Village, a brilliantly made movie about people hiding from the real world because the real world is so foul to them. They succeed in raising their children to be oblivious of the outside world. In the end they maintain their isolation but at a great cost. I think perhaps the best efforts of parents of Empathy to shield children from the world result in a greater handicap. Preparing children to go into the world is a moral obligation, especially for Christianity.

Day 128

I have known an Islamic man. It is the only contact I have ever had with a person of the Islamic faith. He was a young man I coached many years ago. Other than my contact with that young man, my knowledge of Islam is based on readings and what I have learned through media portals. In the grand scheme, my knowledge is rather limited. Being a man of social sciences, I have chosen to read as much as I have been able regarding the religions of the world. Islam does, however, pose unique questions because of the apparent conflict created by world events in the past decade. Most Americans see Islam as a radical religion with ill intentions toward Christianity, and based on media reports, it is hard to dispute. The young man I knew was militant and appeared to wear Islam on his sleeve, but of course, that same description could be administered to many Christians I have known. I have learned through observation that religion is a toxic institution without love. Moreover, it is absent of empathy unless it places love at its core and relationship at its surface. The Islam our nation sees is militant mostly because of the actions of a few. The Christianity the Islamic world sees is arrogant based on the actions of a few. Unfortunately, this is only rectified through education and contact. We owe it to children to teach them world religions in the context of cultural geography and human relations. Without effective education, ignorance will succeed in creating dangerous divides.

Day 129

Where is our mission field? It is here in this school. Every day we are confronted with challenges equal to any that exist in faraway lands. It is not enough to simply teach the obvious. We are bestowed with an opportunity to present ourselves as living examples of faith and beautiful intentions. Children are our mission, and this place is a desolate, empty landscape filled with people in need. Churches present Africa, South America, and Asia as worlds in need, and certainly, this is true, but it is clear to me that our very own homes have fallen victim to a darkness that is just as prevalent as any in the Third World. Yet, because we live in such an apparently affluent society, we grow naïve to the threats all around us. Do not believe mission work is only for those people willing to travel abroad. It is for teachers here.

Day 130

We have a boy attending this school who resembles in many ways a wild animal. His day-to-day affairs are merely acts of survival. He grabs at his food and eats in frantic motions. He tends to be in conflict with other students over space, items, food, and even attention. He exhibits characteristics of neglect. He is seen in town at all hours of the day or night. His parents are noncommittal to any aspect of his education, and upon careful investigation, it is clear they are noncommittal on all aspects of his life. He will not look you in the eyes when you speak to him. His aptitude is quite good, but his academic output is almost nonexistent other than what is drawn from him by a good teacher.

I am reminded of the stray dog ideology. He is not much different than a wild dog running free, trying to survive the day in any way he deems applicable. Perhaps my analogy seems harsh, but it is the truth, and there is not a person in this building that would disagree. Is it not obvious why he fails in school? Is it not obvious why he has relationship issues? Is it not obvious why he cannot find relevance in education? He is a prime candidate for dropping out of school. He is a prime candidate for crime as an adult. He is a prime candidate for dysfunctional relationships as an adult since that is what he is embroiled in now. How can we be okay with this? How can anyone take him personally? He is similar to a Third-World child eating rice from a metal bowl on a dirt floor. His clothes are filthy most of the time. He suffers from body odor. He thinks so little of himself that his mind blocks out the obvious pains of life, and he moves forward like that stray dog on the street looking for the next item of sustenance. Do you see him in the halls? Do you recognize this child?

Day 131

Some people cannot love who they are. They are not comfortable in their own skin. Pay close attention to some students, and you can easily see their insecurities. It is written on their faces, displayed in their actions, and hidden in their words, and we have a choice. We can say they need to grow up or get over their issues, or we can say they must break the cycle or learn to love themselves. Some of us suggest they need to get thicker skin or even cease needing attention and being high maintenance. But I submit to you this morning that without edification from us, those children will not improve unless they have amazing willpower. Few have this inner strength. I think we should assume they couldn't overcome, and proceed with supplying strength to children.

Day 132

There is a bleak reality to emotional pain through the eyes of a child.

Some people learn to cope.

Some learn to expect it because life becomes a series of wounds, and they cannot see any reason to set goals or aspire to something better. The pain is usually associated with how they feel about themselves. In the last journal entry, I wrote about some people not being able to love themselves. Today I examine the pain that causes such issues, and sometimes that pain originates in school. I am an advocate of public education, but only if it is grounded in Christian ideology. It is there we have the best chance of healing people, and it is there we have the best chance of teaching an unclouded mind.

Day 133

We search for God even if we do not realize we are doing so. It is natural to need direction, hope, reward, and security from something greater than our mortal existence. I cannot fathom a universe without a Creator. I notice that children crave structure from adults. Children have an innate need for assurance, and gradually it seems that with maturity it shifts to something higher and higher until life cannot be understood unless we search for God. Every day I watch children interact, learn, survive, and enter into every other possible aspect of living, and in their eyes is the overwhelming need for a higher law or that being that assures justice, fair play, love, rewards, and ultimately safety. We cannot be their God. But we most certainly can show them the way to God. It is done in our actions and words. It is present more so in empathy than any other characteristic of an educator.

Day 134

Communication arts is the beating heart of learning. Imagine, if you will, a man living in the Amazon jungle having never had contact with the outside world. If you encountered him, what would be the first aspect of interaction to take place? Of course, it would be communication. People in educational leadership often forget that language arts are the most imperative aspects of human growth and development. Other subject matters certainly are vital, but the beginning point has to be language arts. Great curriculum revolves around teaching reading and writing. Imagine curriculum as a universe, and communication arts is the sun. All the other subject matters orbit around that reference point. I beg of teachers to place reading and writing at the center of our academic universe.

Day 135

I met a man this past weekend at a Christian men's retreat who described himself as not only born again but also saved by the mercy of another man, his employer. He spoke of how he cheated people, wrote bad checks, used meth and marijuana, and even inadvertently had his wife arrested due to his actions, although she was innocent and loyal. His testimony was the most riveting I have heard at a retreat, and I have attended a multitude. Talking to him later I discovered that he had neglected being educated and could not recall anyone caring that he gave up on life. His description of himself is one I have heard before. I think he represents more people than we realize. I think there is a definitive relationship between uneducated people and the dreadful paths they take. Yes, it is a choice, but that choice is certainly made easier when education is left out of the equation. It was only when he chose Christianity that he began to ascend to a new and amazing life. His employer stayed with him through it all, even funding the bail money for the wife and paying for some of the man's blunders. That employer represents mercy, empathy, and hope. Much like a teacher, he stayed with a person regardless of the heartache until that person found a path toward success and, moreover, redemption.

Day 136

Creativity is at the core of successful teachers. These people do not wait around for ideas or struggle through curriculums, because they are busy exploring resources, and they possess the dynamic personality necessary for powerful interrelationships. Really, this is teaching in the most critical sense. There is no other way to approach the subject. A teacher is an artist, always peering into the potential of subject matter, always observing the pupil and finding the pathways to take to connect. In fact, it is an artistry very much cultivated at a spiritual level, which is why so many people cannot seem to succeed in the profession. Christ possessed a certain flair for storytelling, and His empathy was godly. He connected words with visions, and people around Him were amazed. Of course, the reward was eternal, so every person who heard His message had something to gain by following His instruction. Who has anything to gain from following you? This critical question may be difficult to answer, but search yourself to find it.

Day 137

Let me define a haunted childhood. Can you imagine?

Watching as a father drinks himself into oblivion and the world shakes at the sound of his voice. His words are laced with regret and hatred, for himself upon close examination, but the residual impact is horrid. There is no education in the family other than a few high school diplomas. Several of his aunts and uncles are dropouts. The idea of a person setting a goal is looked upon as foolish. The women in his family are treated as inferiors, spoken harshly to, and placed in a role of humiliating submission. There are drugs as well that seem to surface when money is tight or the fellows get together on weekends.

Adultery has taken place with most of the men he knows, and it seems strange that the women always take them back. The child realizes that if the roles were reversed the women would be called whores. He looks at this paradoxical mindset as part of the ignorance of the men and the oppression of the women.

Poverty is always on the doorstep. There is only enough money to make a meal or drive from here to there. Foul language is the norm. Racism is not hidden. It is revealed at the dinner table, in church, at the school he attends, and moreover, it is spoken of as if the races of the world have only evil intentions toward these Anglo-Saxon, Scotch-Irish hill folks that are convinced their color is ordained.

He is exposed to a sexuality that is marred by selfish minds. And he watches as crimes take place, but he is helpless to do anything about it. He is bullied by adults, and then at school, he is unable to defend himself against harsh words or a blow to his head. He searches for a mentor, but the world has delivered him to himself, and all he can do is learn from his mistakes. Perhaps he will survive to break the cycle.

Do you really think he cares about his grades? Do you really think he is looking toward graduation and possibly higher education?

Teachers should realize their obligation to save this child and help him break free from a world that will choke his hopes if he had any left at the end of the day.

Day 138

Today I must search my soul to find the answers. I have been indifferent to God on certain aspects of life, and I realize I have been selfish. Many of the goals I set are my own, and my intentions are to achieve personal accomplishments or be in charge of my destiny. I have not been a godly man when possessed by that selfishness. I am deeply regretful and came to work this morning in prayer, asking God to forgive me, asking God to clean my mind so I can see clearly that God wants me completely and that all people around me — family, students, teachers, and friends — will benefit from my total surrender. This was not easy to write and then send to all of you. I have been too proud to admit that I have been centered on my own desires of achievement, and I have not been satisfied with where God has placed me. I am sorry. Many of you have heard me make comments about being passed over for a position or not feeling like I was where I was supposed to be, and I am deeply sorry that I allowed my selfishness to obviously control my words. I awoke today with a desire to be open-minded to what God wants and really believe in that, really live it. I hesitated to send this. I even contemplated not journaling for a while, but I realize after praying that it would have been wrong. Every day is a new day.

Day 139

Only the most enlightened administrator can share leadership. I am amazed by the people I have known in leadership positions throughout my life who cannot allow others to invest in the kingship. At the core of every bad leader is a personal quest to be in control totally, and from my viewpoint, a leader who is totally in control is the leader most likely to lose control. People must be allowed a voice in their destinies. This is at the very core of a democratic soul. God wants mankind to reach a place of mutual respect, and leadership can facilitate such an outcome through humility. I pray I never lose my vision of a shared leadership.

Day 140

I have one drop of thought to lend you today.

Water

I have been enamored with streams all of my life. Of course, this began with my introduction to a creek so many years ago. The reason I think of it today is that it rained and I stood in the school hallway, looked outside, and watched it build pools and turn into tiny rivulets as the water began its journey somewhere. No education I have ever experienced meant more to me than the revelation of running water, and even now I find myself learning from it. I would have given anything as a child if a teacher had allowed me to spend any time at all near a stream to collect samples, study insects, photograph scenery, and just allow the drops to etch thoughts in my mind. Do not limit yourself as a teacher to a classroom. There may be a child wishing for another avenue.

Day 141

Today I am reminded of a Scripture that has always spoken to me on the power of love. Christ seemed to use marriage as an example to signify the bond or union of people with God. Ephesians 5:25 tells the Husbands to "love your wives, just as Christ also loved the congregation[12] and gave himself up for her." Jesus loved his followers so much that he suffered one of the most horrendous executions of all time, offering his life as a ransom for them. (Mat. 20:28) Christians husbands and by extension, everyone can imitate Jesus in their unselfish attitude, seeking to please someone other than ourselves, and especially the Father. (Rom. 15:3) A husband should be quick to put the needs of his wife before his own, as a friend should seek to put his or her friend's needs before their own, and so on. The husband should never rigidly insist on having his own way, but he shows a readiness to yield when he sees the reasonableness of his wife's words. The husband, who is eager to show a self-sacrificing love, will find favor with the Father, and he will have the love and respect of his wife and his children. This biblical counsel is something that we all should heed in our lives, with family, friends, schoolmates, coworkers, and so on. I have read and reread this passage often because it makes me feel contented. Can you imagine if all the children we teach daily were coming from homes where they saw a father love a woman to that degree? The problems of the world would be fewer, and most assuredly our lives as educators would be easier.

---

[12] Gr *ekklesia* ("assembly")

Day 142

I have learned that a person can go through tribulation for apparently unseen reasons, until a day in which it is revealed what God's intentions were. I think it is certain that we cannot always know why we endure something, and then suddenly, like waiting for dawn after a long night, we see why we went through it. Today I feel victory or closure over an enigmatic period in my life, and God is glorious through it all. In fact, I am feeling as though I have won a different race, and I pronounce this in all humility. I have developed a new appreciation for God, and why it is vital, we stay the course with our faith and maintain our integrity until that day He reveals to us why the test was necessary. I am reminded that answers do not always arrive in our time, but sometimes we must wait and wait and wait, but therein is the test of faith.

Day 143

In my career as an administrator, I have taken note of an obvious trend. I deal daily with human issues, and over the past decade, I can clearly see that in the vast majority of cases, perhaps 95 percent of the time, I deal with mothers and not fathers. Whether it is a discipline issue or grades, it is the mother who confronts the school or the leadership, and it is the mother who takes the role of communication with the school. Some of the most confrontational moments I have had were with mothers. Fathers show up if it is an athletics issue. However, the athletics aspect is rarer. I could speculate as to why this is the case, but as I look deeper at the whole picture, I see that the roles of men and women have changed so drastically since the early 1980s that it is obvious to me that women are empowered to take this role and men have either given it up or have become uncaring to being the father and taking the lead. No matter the reasons, it is unhealthy to children to watch this reversal take place. Parents should be mutually invested in the education of children. Surely this logic makes sense. In addition, at a godly level, a man is failing by allowing himself to become subordinate.

Day 144

Throughout my years of educational work, I have often been amazed at the sheer level of drama that goes on in a public school. Of course, when you place multitudes of people under one roof, it is bound to happen. That drama is not just confined to kids. The adults participate. If I were to give one remedy to all the problems faced by a school, I would arrive at the simple concept of being nice. There you go. It is the cure-all. The answer to the world's problems and the answer to senior and junior high problems, problems between staff members, issues with parents, issues with public relations, all could be cured by being nice.

Day 145

I just finished reading a chapter from the work of nonfiction by Richard Dowden titled Africa: Altered States, Ordinary Miracles. I was particularly interested in his past as a teacher in Africa and how difficult it was to involve people in education. The various people he encountered were from a crude existence, and getting educated was something they envisioned would relieve them of having to do any more hard work. The Africans he knew labored heavily for their living, and they looked upon education as a way to avoid that hard life.

If you think about it, this is very similar to what people in a rural county think of education for their children. There are exceptions to this, of course, but most people working hard to make it month to month think of an education as a means to escape. It's a shame this is the case because hard work is the reason people succeed. I wonder if some believe that an education is a vessel to get a cushy job and avoid a more industrious life. Either way, it is a complicated cycle that places education as something to remove the concept of hard work and replace it with the façade of an easier life. In reality, an education should be a portal to greater possibilities and accomplishments, which of course leads to a richer life in ways beyond the monetary value.

Day 146

This job is stressful. I need to run or hike daily just to clear my mind. The average person thinks we have it made because our summers are free and holiday vacations are longer than the norm. I joked once to a man who was intent on driving home the point that I had an easy job and plenty of time off by saying to him that I needed the extra time just from having dealt with his kid on a daily basis. He was not amused, and he did not understand my perspective, but I feel my view is dead on. It is a stressful job. I told my wife many times over the years that all it seems I do on a daily basis is take on the role of conflict mediator. Most days I broker some kind of outcome based on another person's bad choices. People are angry, upset, frustrated, and even cynical, and it is the educator who has to find answers. My only response is to turn it over to God, and this is a challenge because driven people wish to be independent and take care of their own problems and those of others. With that in mind, I will meditate today and summon the help of God to take away the stress.

Day 147

Last night I lectured on the concept of diversity as it applies to the field of education. I went home and told my wife I felt I did a poor job teaching the college students because there seemed several thoughts I could not articulate. So many believe diversity means race when in reality it is a word as broad as the spectrum of the human condition. In education, we must understand that literally, every person has diverse needs and diverse traits. The definition of the word is respect. Now that may mean something too simplistic, but if you think deeply about what is required of a teacher, you will see that a true understanding of each child is the foundation of the profession, and in thinking that deeply, we arrive at the truth. Difference is both beautiful and complicated. It asks teachers to create instructional models that are tailored to individualism, and at the same time, that teacher must reach an entire classroom simultaneously. Not an easy job, but nonetheless imperative. Let me restate the obvious. To teach successfully is to possess empathy. To possess empathy is to understand everyone. To understand everyone is to change the world.

Day 148

For reasons that I cannot explain, I miss home. Perhaps I miss the concept of home. My childhood caused a shattering of hope that sent our family in all directions when my grandparents passed away, and it has been nearly three decades since I last went there for any extended period of time. I have passed through on my way elsewhere, and each time I looked at the country roads and old houses as if it were a place I once was but did not want to return to. The river is still green. There are still huge oaks lining the roads, and in the spring, it is the greenest place on earth. Now that I am older, there is something in me that needs to belong to a place. It was strong as a child, and then in the years of adulthood, I grew so distant from that childhood home that I was sure I would never desire to go back. And now it is a growing emotion, this need for home. I think it is a fire burning in every child. There is something inherently beautiful about feeling at home. I miss Arkansas. Yes, it was a place of turmoil and pains, but even a broken family loves through the wreckage, and it endures. A person can never really shake loose or wash away the dust and stains of home. No matter how long it has been or how far we are from the places that defined our youth, we are always tied or bound to those places. Human beings are a strange species indeed. We compile memories, images of the past, holding on to that which we deem soothing to our sanity and hiding those that threaten it.

Day 149

Last night I was engrossed in a documentary about war photographer James Nachtwey. This man has spent his life photographing some of the most horrific human catastrophes, ranging from combat to famine, and his images are sobering, disturbing, and possibly enlightening, if you can see his work with your soul. There is one image of a person in Africa dying of starvation, crawling on a dirt road, a body reduced to limbs of twigs, and in that image is all that is wrong with our Church. Perhaps I am too cynical, but I felt something empty about where we are as a culture as I observed that image. In America, we talk about the economy and live as if money was the chief reason to vote for a presidential candidate. We live in a culture that offers us imagery of violence, sexuality, money, and reality shows, and lost in the myriad of immorality is the simple fact that atrocities are occurring all over the world every day. We literally watch from a distance, only engaging in their world through the media and sometimes for mere seconds. This photographer jolted me. As I watched, I was feeling the urge to help, and yet all I could do was watch. I pray every day for the strength to help others, and sometimes I wonder if I am doing enough. I hope my prayers and empathy somehow reaches across the oceans. Educators owe it to children to show them the painful realities that exist in our broken world, and we must do more than simply talk about it. As painful as the images were, I think children need to see them.

Day 150

At one point in my career, I was a losing college basketball coach, doing so badly that I am certain no other program was as pitiful. Even now as I look back, I cannot shake the feeling that I was to blame wholesale. I recruited the players and formed the team, and although there were circumstances that did not help matters, I was nonetheless the man in charge, and we lost miserably, and often. It was an era in my life that can be described as training.

I realize now that some of the best instruction and coachings I ever did was during that long span of three years and the run of losses that was suffered. My real regret is for those young men I coached. I can still see their faces and feel their dejection. In fact, I think of them often and wish I could call them, each and everyone, and apologize for that period of time. I wonder where they all are and if they learned anything from me.

Last night I could not sleep, and I sat on the front porch thinking of those student-athletes and hoping they found some peace of mind. Never think that losing is not a sorrowful experience if it becomes a habit. I realize now with maturity that tough experiences somehow make us better people, but the sting is no less because of this realization. My pain is not for me but for them. In education, and coaching as well, we are responsible for so much, and we should regret the failures of our pupils as if those were our own. I think I have learned that taking ownership of another person's misfortunes and blunders in the learning process creates a deeper empathy within us as teachers. I can only hope that I have articulated my thoughts in this writing, because at a deep level, this concept I share is so very crucial to becoming a complete teacher.

Day 151

I must learn to stop saying "me."

As it relates to education, we must not say "I" or "me." A school is a shared ideology, a shared leadership, a shared learning experience, a shared culture, and a shared goal. I recall when I was younger and trying to find my way in this profession, I viewed a team I coached as "my team" and a classroom as "my kids," and it seemed that I was speaking of them as if I so dearly loved them all and wanted to be in control; but at a deep level, this is simply a type of selfishness. Yes I was the leader, but my success was insignificant compared to theirs, and, moreover, it was their success that mattered most, if not completely. We must share all aspects in a way that creates a culture of us and not me.

Day 152

The concept of an at-risk student is not something new to educators, but it seems to me that after countless years of scrutinizing the idea, many teachers are no closer to understanding what it takes to reach that student. In fact, I am more and more unimpressed with the lack of patience and lack of compassion demonstrated by some people in education. Most discipline problems that occur with an at-risk student occur when the adult is confrontational. I realize this may not be the case always, and I realize it is a perspective that might indeed lead a teacher to think that I am blaming the adult, but what I really mean to indicate is that a student more often than not will react to a relationship in a positive manner as opposed to reacting to a confrontation in a negative manner.

The reality is quite simple. You cannot take kids personally. If you look deeply at the soul, who they could be, or will be, then you begin to see a project worth working on. It is the teacher who takes everything personally that fails to reach children. Christ taught in a way that He did not take sinful nature personal. In fact, He expected people to be imperfect, and He addressed that aspect with great empathy and patience. He knew humanity was flawed. He approached mankind with the intention of serving. Now I realize this is a strange ideology to the teacher who expects kids to simply follow directives without problematic results. We must serve children. We must appear Christlike in that regard. It is only through a servant's mentality that we reach a child who sometimes refuses to be helped.

Day 153

He suffers from attention deficit disorder. His learning is hampered by clearly defined mental issues. In fact, there is striking evidence he once suffered from mild schizophrenia and obsessive-compulsive behaviors. There are bouts of serious paranoia from time to time, noted by a doctor. Medication has been applied, but with negative results. He has the tendency to create alter worlds and thought processes to cope with reality. His parents are divorcing. He is exposed to drug and alcohol abuse. He has witnessed a multitude of domestic violence episodes, including the beating of his mother. He has been beaten and verbally abused. He has been exposed to pornography and gambling at a young age. One of his parents dropped out of school before the tenth grade, and the family as a whole places no merit on education at any level. His learning is impeded because of obvious emotional issues. He struggles to form relationships. He has blatant issues with male authority.

Who is this student?

Me.

Day 154

Over the past ten years, I have sat through countless administrative meetings and listened to the magic number of 95. That number represents the attendance percentage that seems to be the coveted mark we as leaders should be striving for to have top-notch attendance. Any number above 95 is considered outstanding, and any number below seems to begin the process of worry. In fact, 93 percent is terrible, depending on who you talk to, and 96 percent is amazing, depending on who you talk to.

In the last ten years, our attendance seems to hover around 94 or 95 percent. We have tried every tactic known to educational leadership to increase that percentage, and it seems we cannot get too high or too low. I call it a statistical monster that cannot be swayed by rewards and incentives. I think that monster is trying to get us to take a closer look at the five percent that fall through our average daily attendance nets. I think that five percent is representative of all that is wrong with the world. In the arena of education, it seems there are

Five kids out of a hundred who stand by the road saying they will work for food. Those same five kids are also those that end up in prison or perhaps die young or live to an old age with no home. In other words, we worry as an institution about the ninety-five percent, and it is the other five percent that seem faceless to us. I am not sure who they are. I'm not even sure I could create a theory as to how we can identify them, but if we are prudent about the culture of our school and creating empathy, then surely that five percent will be included.

Day 155

I thought yesterday about a concept that Christians sometimes behave differently once they are saved, so to speak. What I mean is that people, for the most part, live their lives on a journey in which they blunder, trip, fall, get dirty, and call that "life experience," even if it is a resume they wished never had been created. Through those times they form who they are to become, and then the transformation takes place. They become Christians, and they are born again, saved, and transformed. It is supposed to be the beginning of a new life in Christ. But what seems to happen is the creation of stringent boundaries and new laws to live by. Suddenly their desire to be clean makes them look at their past life as utterly filthy and regretful.

Bear in mind that we should all feel terrible about our mistakes and bad choices, but it is clear to me that "becoming new" means to forgive yourself and dissolve the past indiscretions. It means to be happy or content and move on. Our new morality should not make us forlorn and so heavenly focused that we are of no earthly good. In addition, we should be teaching children how to move on and not dwell on past mistakes. In fact, I am afraid some in education dwell on who a child was the year before, and begin each year expecting more difficulties. We cannot through pious means turn our faith into something so polished that people liked us better when we were pagans.

Day 156

I like the motto we have developed here in this school. "Just roll with it." It simply means that we shouldn't take anything personally, and repair whatever is broken, because things are going to break. Instead of standing around pointing fingers or talking about how or why something broke, we have a moral obligation to have the backs of our colleagues and step up to help repair whatever needs repairing. I think the overall mood of a school culture is greatly enhanced if everyone feels they are being treated with loyalty and support. In fact, I am sure it is something very much needed by all parties involved. So if a student drops a tray or the bells stop working, or the roof is leaking, or a parent has just verbally shredded the front office, or someone forgets something, or the smart board light bulb goes out, or, or, or. . . .

Just roll with it because it takes more character to help with a smile than it does to add to the woes.

Day 157

What is the purpose of education? Is it to teach the fundamentals of school, such as reading, writing, mathematics, science, etc.? Of course there is no education without those fundamentals, but there is one fundamental at the core of the human condition that is paramount to our success as individuals long before we take seriously all those other facets of curriculum. It is the word character, and though I have touched on this in many of my past journal entries, today I am confronted by the image of a major college figurehead making millions in a high-profile athletic position, and it was his lack of integrity that ultimately cost him. So it is that in spite of how highly he was trained, or how intelligent he may be, his single-most-critical characteristic proved to be his weakest. We are all guilty of character flaws, and we have all been perpetrators in our lives. To suggest otherwise is arrogant. We as educators must take seriously the character and integrity of children long before we take on the obvious academic areas of emphasis.

Day 158

Just a thought. . . .

We took the sixth-grade boys to the zoo this morning, and one of our at-risk students spent nearly an hour feeding a baby camel. Twice I asked him if he was okay and if he would like to move around the grounds and see the other animals. Both times, he calmly replied that he was enjoying himself and he liked the new friend he had made. This boy is always quiet in school and tends to worry about his conduct by informing me and others fairly often that he is being good. I wonder if he is told fairly often that he is bad and that is why he tends to fixate on his conduct. Either way, I am certain that camel may be the only living thing in his world that does not judge him, at least in his eyes.

Day 159

I'm not sure how to articulate this.

I am troubled by leadership that does not participate in the teaching/learning process. I feel confident that many leaders take on the role because they did not want to teach anymore and they soon forget how tough the job is. I believe a person needs to teach at least five years before they can be considered for administrative work. And once they are in a leadership role they should willingly take on educational roles such as supervision, and I do not mean ballgames only. I mean take on supervision of field trips, classrooms, activity time, etc. . . .

As you already know, I believe in shared leadership, and this means I wish to feel as though I am still a teacher. Without that feeling, I am nothing more than a facilitator of events who tells the real teachers what to do.

Day 160

Can we create students who feel entitled? Parents create children of this nature and schools inherit the problem, and sometimes it's vice versa. Do you know someone who literally needs every aspect of life repaired, or do they constantly need counsel with problems? Why is it that people of this nature cannot seem to function unless someone else is taking care of every need or issue? I think our children have learned to be enabled by a society that teaches them that independence is not a life skill. Our youth have grown up in a world that does not value goal setting or hard work. Instead, our youth are part of the mindset of, "If it's difficult, it's not worth doing," or "I would rather someone else take care of it because I can't." I think our youth need to develop the good feeling that comes upon the soul that can stand on its own two feet and possesses self-discipline. There is power in independence. Our children can survive and even flourish if they possess independence.

Day 161

Yesterday a father sat across from me as I addressed his son's conduct, and I realized that boy is so very mired in a pitiful situation — so much so that all the good efforts of educators are countered by the home environment and personal helplessness of a parent. This man looked and behaved as if he had nothing left to live for. He sat quietly as I spoke, and gradually I began to feel as if I was being redundant and my words were just falling on deaf ears. He was respectful but clearly apathetic and unable to help himself, much less his son. I think perhaps we do not realize the scope of the problems encountered by at-risk children if their parents are also at-risk. I even made the statement to the father that I felt all of our best efforts were being countered when the student was not with us. I was trying to diplomatically state that parenting or lack thereof was working against our educational goals for his son, but my subtle hint was lost in his blank stare. There is no doubt in my mind that we are working against a darkness that is strong and motivated. Our efforts must be passionate.

Day 162

Is there a way to teach children to need God? And if so, how is that defined or how can we articulate such a concept? We teach children so many life lessons and aspects, but do we really teach them to need God? I think it begins by teaching them to search for God in every facet of their existence. I realize this is an abstract viewpoint that could be discussed endlessly, but really it could be reduced to a simple ideology if you think about it. To need God is to want morality and decency in your life. It is the inherent trust in the moral and natural laws that dictate the universe, and we all must have faith that a benevolent being, our God, put this spectacular system into motion, and we are a grand part of the plan. From there, children are easily mentored because they see order in life and know it is God. We all need God, even if we do not always realize it. It is a natural part of the human condition. We are inquisitive and yearning to find answers. God is there just beyond our mortal scope, and this can be offered to children in a classroom setting as easily as mathematics, literature, or science. Once we establish the reality of God, we can venture further, and our Christianity becomes apparent and believable.

Day 163

I feel that if we are angry in an issue then we are selfish. What I mean is this. A parent called wanting a bus issue resolved, and she grew angry because the dialogue she was having was not what she wanted to hear. Then she grew angrier and hung up the telephone. When people are confronted with conflict resolution, more often than not they choose self-preservation over humility. It is natural if our lives are godless, because, without God, we cannot possess empathy or the ability to meet someone in the middle of an issue. You have heard the expression to "pick your battles." I would submit to you that you are a better man or woman if you can diffuse the battle altogether through humble compromise. If you feel that you are having to compromise your morals, then you could still diffuse the battle through humility. People who must win every argument are those who are selfish. Sometimes there is honor in giving yourself up. People tend to look at that as something powerful and righteous. It is a gift from God and supernatural.

Day 164

Do you make good choices? Are you disciplined and able to carry on your daily life, keeping things in moderation and under control, and do you lead by example? When children or adults look at you, do they get a good impression? If you answered no to any of these questions, are you really qualified to teach? I think of a college basketball official running up and down the court, always two seconds behind the action, unable to keep his shirt tucked in, his face unshaven, and his clothes not coordinated. Can the teams and coaches really expect his game judgment to be on the mark consistently if his personal judgment is so poor? I think my analogy has merit. If we cannot take care of ourselves, then how can we be charged with the imperative responsibility of taking care of children? Who are we to judge if we are poor examples?

Day 165

I was in the mall a few days ago, and as I sat down to have lunch in the food court, I noticed a woman in a wheelchair seated alone at a table. There were people all around. She was facing a plate of food, and she sat patiently, unable to feed herself. I stopped eating. She was smallish and literally helpless. I cannot say what her condition was, but it was obvious she needed someone and was waiting for someone. I grew teary eyed thinking of what it must be like to live your life knowing you cannot do anything for yourself and you rely one hundred percent on another, even to feed you. In time, a woman came to the table with her own food, and before she began to eat, she prepared to feed the helpless woman. She carefully fed her, and then would take her own bite. They smiled at each other and exchanged no dialogue other than smiles. Their gestures and facial expressions spoke a million words. And it was at that moment that I did an inventory of my own life. Who would feed me? Whom would I feed? Could I smile through such circumstances? I can only assume the woman who did the feeding is a Christian. And if she is, then most assuredly she is close to God, being the servant she is. How long would any of us wait sitting in front of our lunch, hungry, before someone fed us? How long would someone else wait for us to feed them?

Day 166

Teaching and learning is a complex process, but we need not create complications. Through simplistic ideologies, we can create an ideal school culture and in turn create successful people. I sat at my computer this morning formulating thoughts for my college students and wanted to include in my journal a simple summation of what I believe is crucial to a successful school culture.

Let me begin by stating I am confident, through years of experience, that education is best accomplished with the creation of an ideal culture. There are three imperative aspects to address.

Student Conduct

Education is nonexistent if a teacher lacks classroom management skills. In addition, a building leader must be at the forefront of student conduct through high expectations and accountability. A school culture is only as healthy as the moral code established by leadership and maintained by all stockholders, and this includes the community. A school district must collaborate with the community and build the ideal public relations model. Each member of a school district has a moral obligation to set and uphold exemplary standards of conduct and to create measures of accountability. In addition, staff members, teachers, and administration must lead by example. It is godly people who get godly results.

Dynamic Teachers

There is no way a college can prepare you to become a teacher. It is those people who possess a myriad of personality traits and skills that cultivate learning. I submit to you what I believe to be the imperative seven.

(1) Empathy

(2) Communication

(3) Enthusiasm

(4) Creativity

(5) Knowledge in content area

(6) Technologically adapted

(7) A lifelong learner

Progressive Curriculum

This begins with a commitment to literacy. Reading and writing are at the core of student learning and are the pulse to determine success or failure. I am constantly stating that if we accomplish only one goal as educators, it must be to graduate literate people. Literacy can be applied across all content areas and all grades. We must also realize that we as educators are no longer solely in possession of knowledge. With the broad potential of technology and the Internet, students are capable of becoming enlightened. A challenge has emerged for teachers to not only become facilitators but to also become motivators. This new door opened by technology has also created informed parents. We must become open to the idea of web-based curriculums. Finally, we should realize the need to teach vast perspectives to children, to create grading methodologies that reflect true learning, be sensitive to diversity, and be open to change, always realizing our world is perpetually evolving.

Day 167

Do you realize the immense power in the word love? Does the word leave your mouth like any other word? Do you really feel love, or is it like any other emotion, coming and going like anger, hate, pity, jealousy, or sadness? My eyes are like windows to something difficult to put into words, but I will try. Love to me is the power of eternal thought. It is a word to describe God when all else seems to fall short. I believe we are capable of loving beyond mortal feelings and that our love can endure anything, even death. I believe in the words of love songs, the prince carrying away the princess, the poet writing of something all-consuming, and the first and last lines in the David Gates song, "The Goodbye Girl."

All your life you've waited for love to come and stay.

Cause now you're home at last.

We all are born to search for it. Great is the man or woman who really does find it. Sorrow follows those who do not. It was my prayer for my children that they should someday find their soulmate. Life is so very empty without believing in love, without feeling it. I need to believe in the unbelievable, and certainly, the truest love is not of this world. We cannot take this word lightly in our day-to-day affairs. Empathetic people feel this. They relate to what I have written in this journal. Do not use the word unless you believe in God, because they are one and the same.

Day 168

Dysfunctional people attract dysfunctional people.

I write these words today as a reminder that if we are unable to overcome that which controls us then surely, we are destined to pass it on to others or, moreover, create others like ourselves. This is logic. You do not need a university study to arrive at these conclusions. A drunk is likely to cause a ripple effect. A drug user is likely to cause a ripple effect. An ignorant person is likely to cause a ripple effect. You surely get the idea. You have also surely heard the phrase "break the cycle." Breaking that cycle is hard for children because their parents have such a profound influence on them. It is only through God that we achieve any liberation from what constrains our hopes. I have said many times in classes I have instructed that education is the portal for a person to see clearly an escape from the cycle. However, I really should have said that God is the portal.

Day 169

I can still vividly see the porch light at my grandparents' home in the warm evenings of spring. The river was close by, and sometimes at night I would sit on the porch and watch the mayflies gather around the light. In my youth, I was perplexed by the search for God. The legalism of church was a stark contrast to the God in my heart. I just could not believe what church was telling me, but my heart was speaking a clear language. And that porch light gave me comfort. I began to formulate the idea that our souls are like those mayflies, seeking to fly to a light, a warm light, and I wondered if that is what God really is. I think the souls that find God fly to the light and are comforted forever and those that do not are left to wander in the darkness. My analogy may be childish, but if you think deeply about the complexity of life and the mystery of creation, you arrive at places that are incomprehensible. I can recall staring at the light and the mayflies for hours as I sat in a porch chair. I recently told my wife that our lives are like those mayflies. I related this to her and then told her that my love for her is much like finding that light and finding God. If this seems a random thought leading nowhere, then I can only apologize that I fell short of penning my thoughts. However, imagine being a mayfly, short-lived and struggling in the dark.

Day 170

Imagine if you will that every child was a nation, and each child was either a developed nation or an underdeveloped nation, or perhaps a Third-World nation is a better term. In our building, there are 420 nations. They are all different, coming from different cultures. Some are similar, and some are so radically different that the gulf between having it all and having nothing is wider than most people can comprehend. And therein is a complex problem that creates conflict that is sometimes unresolved.

If a developed child and a Third-World child arrive at a problem, the solutions are predictable for the most part. The developed child has been more than likely subjected to educated and/or motivated parents and is provided with relationship tools. Therefore, conflict is a manageable concept. The Third-World child is more likely to fight, to struggle for life because he or she has been denied the basics and has not been around educated people for the most part. These children's lives are not much different than those people of Third-World nations who exist in poverty, are drawn into dogmatic and insensible beliefs, and are governed by powers that do not foster individual growth and freedoms. There are exceptions to the rule, of course, but if you understand the cultural differences between children in a school, then you have a good grasp of why the less developed child struggles to resolve conflict. It may also be worth considering the same principles apply to why there are such vast differences between nations of the world.

Day 171

I can recall being a little boy in the church of my youth and thinking.

I hear you preaching. I hear your words. I understand your intent. So you think you know God. You think you know Jesus? I hear you talking about salvation and the threats of eternal damnation. I hear you telling me that you know how to get to heaven. I hear you talking about the drunk or the criminal and how they had better shape up or be shipped out. I hear you saying you have the answers because you read the Bible and watch the televangelists. Let me explain something to you. The Jesus I know had no time for hard wooden pews in stuffy buildings where men in cheap suits speak of relationships with God and lecture others on exactly how much money they needed to give so the kingdom would progress.[13]

The Jesus I know did not condone the talking spiritualist. He loved the doer. He loved the person who did not seek success but instead sought significance. The Jesus I know walked beside a sea. He prayed in a garden. He was immersed in water. He walked throughout the land searching for those in need. He healed the sick. He readily gave mercy as if it were water for the thirsty. The Jesus I know talked about the birds of the fields, and He appreciated flowers having more beauty than anything Solomon could conjure. The Jesus I know talked about faith like that of a child, and moreover, He loved the childlike believer. I think He would appreciate a dreamer.

The Jesus I know ate with the people who had no one to eat with them. The Jesus I know did not have time for loud talkers in the temples where the offering plate shone like temptation. He was too busy walking the land searching for lost sheep. He reached out a hand to the lowly and declared them meek, saying they would inherit the earth. In this day and age, where men are macho and try to conquer the world, I am at peace knowing that to inherit the world does not require arrogant traits but instead requires humility.

---

[13] **CPH:** This paragraph is not to suggest that all Christian leaders are of this sort. However, many spend more time worrying about how much is coming in through contributions than feeding their flock spiritually. Nevertheless, there are Christian leaders out there that are working very hard in order to care for their flock. In addition, this paragraph is not suggesting that Christian meeting are not important and Jesus would have never suggested such a thing. In fact, the apostle Paul commanded us to attend Christian meetings.

The Empathy Chronicles

The Jesus I know said, "Go and sin no more." He did not lecture the sinner about the sin.[14] He simply requested change, and that scares people who are intent on placing blame, finding scapegoats, or producing litigation. He scares the arrogant. In addition, they should be scared. I think Jesus would sit quietly beside the still waters or lie in the tall prairie grass to rest after He had walked the land searching for those lost sheep. I think He would drink spring waters and say that indeed His Father was the greatest scientist the universe has ever known and that we should stop wondering how the universe was formed and just accept the fact that miracles are as real as creation.

The perfect example — what if students said this about their teachers?

---

[14] CPH: In the Scriptures, "sin" and "sinners" usually refers to one who is living a life of sin. Jesus did actually let those who were sinners, namely, living in sin know what their outcome was going to be. He did condemn sinners quite regularly. I believe the author here is using hyperbole to say that Jesus main message was not how bad of a person you are, what a great sinner you are but rather one of hope and an opportunity at salvation.

Day 172

Why are people at their best at a retirement dinner or a funeral? Why is it that we save our edification for those leaving us or the deceased? It seems to me that Christians should be at the forefront of edification and should not wait until we find ourselves at a retirement party or funeral, spilling out words that we could not say or refused to say when we had the chance. Adults are just as likely to speak ill of their peers behind their backs as any middle-school child is. In fact, some of the worst gossip and drama happens in the teachers' lounge. We owe it to our colleagues and people in general to think positively and speak positively. In the end, there will be no words saved for moments of hypocrisy.

Day 173

Can a life be ruined in one moment? Is it possible a child could think this because peer pressure is that strong?

Children sometimes look back on mistakes as if they had sold their souls, and the scars of those mistakes are still evident in adulthood. I have witnessed moments in the lives of children when words or actions leave them utterly destitute and reeling. Recovering from being struck by a bully or being slandered by peers is sometimes all that is needed to lead a child down a pathway of guilt that stays long after graduation. We have an obligation to teach courtesy. It is a concept spoken of in Titus 3:2, where we are instructed to use perfect courtesy. I would define that concept as acute empathy. Our ability to be empathetic leads us to perfect courtesy and no scars.

Day 174

School consumed 12 years of my life. I sat alone a few nights ago under the stars thinking about those 12 years, and I tried to come up with 12 memories. Much to my consternation, I could only produce negative thoughts.

First grade: Someone shoved me over a kid on the playground, and all the boys laughed at me.

Second grade: A teacher accused me of cheating and stood me in front of the class to get a confession.

Third grade: A teacher told my mother I was slower than the other kids and she could not help me.

Fourth grade: My test scores were awful, and I struggled to improve. It was pointed out many times by teachers.

Fifth grade: Someone shoved me into a bookshelf from behind, and I bled all over the room and wept pitifully.

Sixth grade: I lost a costume contest, and the teacher singled me out as looking silly. I wept. She was mean.

Seventh grade: I went to a dance and embarrassed myself by dancing for the first time. I never danced in school again.

Eighth grade: I was beat up by a bully. He was bigger than me, and he literally had me in fear daily. I heard he had been in jail.

Ninth grade: I was moved to varsity baseball to start at catcher, and in the state tournament, a coach humiliated me in front of the team. I felt such animosity toward him that I cannot put it into words. In fact, to this day I have not been that humiliated.

Tenth grade: I faked a football injury so I could stop playing for a coach. I am still haunted by that cowardly choice I made.

Eleventh grade: I did not play football because of a coach. I am still haunted by that cowardly choice I made.

Twelfth grade: I blatantly disrespected a teacher. I am still haunted by that cowardly choice I made.

You decide if these memories were character builders.

Day 175

I recall being a small boy, perhaps age five, and I was forced to attend Sunday school in Jonesboro, Arkansas, on a hot summer night. I think it was vacation Bible school. Do you remember those days? I sat in a room with kids I did not know, listening to a teacher, I had never met, and suddenly I was filled with anxiety and fear. I have no idea why, but in an instant, I bolted from the room and ran down a long hallway and out the door into a humid July evening. I ran up Fisher Street in the dark as if I were being chased by a lion. I entered our house, and my mother just calmly asked me what I was doing home and did not make me go back. I recall feeling the same way in first grade, but the run would have been twelve miles, and I did not feel I could succeed. I remember that fearful feeling, and I would not wish it on anyone. I think it is possible a middle school or high school student could feel that way the first day.

Day 176

I read a quote by the late author Walker Percy: "You can make As and still flunk life."[15] The man was so right. Teachers must bear in mind that academic success pales in comparison to spiritual success. I am certain a child led by moral and loving people will have a greater chance at success regardless of academic successes or failures. Intellect is only as good as it is ethical.

---

[15] Walker Percy, The Second Coming (New York: Farrar, Straus and Giroux, 1980).

Day 177

On this last day of school, I feel exasperated by meetings that seem negative in context and go on for hours. I vow that if I am ever in a position to save another person from this environment, I will. An educational leader who has received an advanced degree from a diploma mill program and now must have an audience to bore into self-doubt convinces me that hell is a PowerPoint presentation. But this is not me. I am a teacher first and an administrator second. I love the pursuit of truth and then the process of delivering that truth to students. I watched today as our children left us for the summer. I wonder how they will change in the short season between now and the beginning of another school year. As the buses roll away, I am reminded how important this profession really is, and how honored we should all feel about working to mold and even save lives. I too feel like a child knowing that I have a summer in front of me. May God bless us all with eternally perfect summers.